WOMEN
—OF—
PURPOSE

*Inspirational Stories of Professional Women
For Insight and Direction*

WOMEN OF INFLUENCE

This publication is designed to provide competent and reliable information regarding the subject matter covered. However, it is sold with the understanding that the authors and the publisher are not engaged in rendering legal, financial, accounting, or other professional advice. Laws and practices often vary from state-to-state and if legal, financial, or other expert assistance is required, the services of a professional should be sought. The authors and publisher specifically disclaim any liability that is incurred from the use or application of the contents of this book.

Copyright © 2018 Higgins Publishing. All rights reserved.
Women of Purpose: Inspiring Stories of Professional Women for Insight and Direction

---

Higgins Publishing supports the rights to free expression and the value of copyright. The purpose of copyright is to encourage writers and artists to produce the creative works that enrich our values. The scanning, uploading, and distribution of this book without express permission of the publisher is a theft of intellectual property. If you would like permission to use material from this book (other than for review purposes), please contact permissions@higginspublishing.com. Thank you for your support of copyright law.

Higgins Publishing | www.higginspublishing.com

The publisher is not responsible for websites (or their content) that are not owned by the publisher.

Higgins Publishing is committed to excellence in the publishing industry. The company reflects the philosophy established by the founder, based on Psalm 68:11, *"The Lord gave the word, and great was the company of those who published it."*

Unless otherwise noted Scriptures are from the Holy Bible, English Standard Version), copyright 2001 by Crossway, a publishing ministry of Good News Publishers. Used by permission. All rights reserved. Scriptures marked (KJV) are taken from the King James Version of the Bible.

Scripture quotations marked (NKJV) are from the New King James Version. Copyright 1982 by Thomas Nelson. Used by permission. All rights reserved.

Library of Congress Cataloging-in-Publication Data
Co-Author & Compiler Higgins, Shanene - *Women of Purpose: Inspiring Stories of Professional Women for Insight and Direction*

Higgins Publishing First Softcover Edition August 2018
pages cm.   Control Number: 2018940389
Includes Index

Collaborating Co-Authors: Dr. Najah A. Barton, Jazmine Blake, Vanessa Brown, Veronica Clanton-Higgins, Alexandria Cunningham, Nikeisha Darensburg, Benta Davis, Judy Davis, Chontae Edison, Rashell Evans, Incredible Faith, Nealy Gihan, Dr. Sandra Hamilton (Hill), Tasha Huston, Leona Johnson, Nora Macias, Leandra McLaurin, Shirlyon McWhorter, Michele Mills, Dr. Ngozi M. Obi, Beverly Reynolds, Tiffany Richards, Jasmine Spratt-Clarke, Shaunic Stanford, Quinn Thompson, Emem Washington, Dr. Michelle K. Watson, Dr. Pamela R. Wiggins, Erin Williams, and Deborah Young.

ISBN: 978-1-941580-42-4 (softcover) * 978-1-941580-44-8 (hardcover)
978-1-941580-43-1 (e-book) * 978-1-941580-45-5 (companion journal)

1. (REL012040) Religion: Christian Life – Inspirational
2. (SEL021000) Self-Help: Motivational & Inspirational
3. (SEL016000) Self-Help: Personal Growth - Happiness

For information about special discounts for bulk purchases, subsidiary, foreign and translations rights contact Higgins Publishing at sales@higginspublishing.com.

TABLE OF CONTENTS

INTRODUCTION IX

CHAPTER 1 11
Finding Her 11
By Dr. Najah A. Barton 11

CHAPTER 2 15
Keep on Living 15
By Jazmine Blake 15

CHAPTER 3 21
The Inseparable Sustainer 21
By Vanessa Brown 21

CHAPTER 4 25
Girl, Breathe! 25
By Veronica Clanton-Higgins 25

CHAPTER 5 29
No Plan? No Problem! 29
By Alexandria Cunningham 29

CHAPTER 6 35
This Was It! 35
By Nikeisha Darensburg 35

CHAPTER 7 41
Finding the Strength 41
By Benta Davis 41

TABLE OF CONTENTS

CHAPTER 8 45
LIFE IN WORDS 45
BY JUDY DAVIS 45

CHAPTER 9 49
OVERCOMING ABUSE 49
BY CHONTAE EDISON 49

CHAPTER 10 53
MAKING A STATEMENT FOR LOVE 53
BY RASHELL EVANS 53

CHAPTER 11 57
MARATHON RUNNER 57
BY INCREDIBLE FAITH 57

CHAPTER 12 63
A LEAP FROM FEAR TOWARD PURPOSE 63
BY NEALY GIHAN 63

CHAPTER 13 67
GETTING MY LOVE IN ORDER 67
BY DR. SANDRA HAMILTON (HILL) 67

CHAPTER 14 71
BEHIND A VEIL 71
BY SHANENE HIGGINS 71

CHAPTER 15 75
GO! 75
BY TASHA HUSTON 75

CHAPTER 16 79

Redefining Your Purpose 79
By Leona Johnson 79

Chapter 17 83
Nothing is Wasted 83
By Nora Macias 83

Chapter 18 87
Girl, Me Too! 87
By Leandra McLaurin 87

Chapter 19 91
No Matter the Circumstances 91
By Shirlyon McWhorter 91

Chapter 20 95
A Heart that Forgives 95
By Michele Mills 95

Chapter 21 101
The Journey to Purpose 101
By Dr. Ngozi M. Obi 101

Chapter 22 105
Chasing A Dream 105
By Beverly Reynolds 105

Chapter 23 109
The Meeting Place 109
By Tiffany Richards 109

Chapter 24 113
She Chose Purpose 113

TABLE OF CONTENTS

By Jasmine Spratt-Clarke 113

CHAPTER 25 117
Her Freedom 117
By Shaunic Stanford 117

CHAPTER 26 121
Who Am I? 121
By Quinn Thompson 121

CHAPTER 27 127
Flip the Page! 127
By Emem Washington 127

CHAPTER 28 131
Rebecca at the Well: Should She Water or Doppler the Dromedaries? 131
By Dr. Michelle K. Watson 131

CHAPTER 29 137
Breaking Down Barriers 137
By Dr. Pamela R. Wiggins 137

CHAPTER 30 141
Blossoming into my Purpose 141
By Erin Williams 141

CHAPTER 31 145
A Rose from the Concrete 145
By Deborah Young 145

INDEX 149

ABOUT THE AUTHORS 161

TABLE OF CONTENTS

WOP CHAPTER REGISTRATION 213

WOP PRODUCTS 217

FEATURED ADVERTISERS 225

INTRODUCTION

WE OFTEN go through life on autopilot, completing one task after another, not reflecting upon what we are purposed or even called to do. It is not until we make the conscious decision to change our current situation for the better that real change occurs. However, change without opposition is often an anomaly and most likely does not come easy. Regardless of the challenges that we face, greatness requires tenacity, courage, consistency, a made-up mind, academic achievements, and faith that all things are possible with God! Thus, the purpose of this book is to help you reflect upon the inspiring and transparent true stories written by professinal and influential women who desire to help you reach your God-ordained purpose. As you reflect upon the stories, you may find yourself written within the pages of this book as you laugh, cry, and even rejoice with the authors as they share their pain, happiness, challenges, triumphs, and successes. We pray that you will glean enough hope to take a step or even a leap of faith, to do what you have been created to do and make a positive impact on the world through touching the lives of girls and women worldwide.

CHAPTER 1

FINDING HER
BY DR. NAJAH A. BARTON

Self. Singleness. Success. Three attributes earned—not given. The appreciation of these facts today, did not come without trials and tribulations. To reflect on a single moment in time that contributed to finding 'herself,' embracing her 'singleness,' and being humbled by her ability to reach 'success' has not been easy. Why; you might ask? Because the mass dimensions that encompass her came with a lot—bad and good. So much so that the bad always appeared to outweigh the good—yes, even when a lot of good followed.

There were several failed or dead-end relationships that led to her being forced to learn and understand what it meant to truly be happy. With a healthy self-concept and image, she is able to identify with her past. From humble beginnings, she grew up in the inner city of New York City with a single mother who worked endless hours to provide for her daughters. All the while, as the youngest of two, she succumbed to societal pressures, engaging in promiscuous behaviors, ran the streets, hung out with friends rather than taking her education seriously, and worse of all, lashing out too many times to count with rage and anger fits towards her mother because she blamed her mother for not having her father. She recalled an incident that occurred at the age of two when her father and mother were arguing, and her father pushed her mother, which led her [mom] to fall over a glass table. This, amongst other incidences, contributed to her mother leaving her father. However, she could not understand that. To most recently relocating with two suitcases and her dog, Bella from the West to East Coast of the United States for employment, and because it was her then husband's next desired location in his military career—only to be told less than 30 days after leaving her home and over the phone, "I want a divorce."

To tell 'her' life's story in its entirety is not possible, herein. Rather, this chapter serves as a glimpse of how important *'Finding Her,'* and being happy in her singleness and success, have aided her in *Becoming her Best Self*! The best parts of her are defined through her work as an educator, being a helping professional, leading and managing change, completing research on behalf of those who cannot or have not been able to advocate for themselves, and owning the fact of being a survivor. Additionally, she is an honorably discharged veteran and has decided, through a long spiritual and enlightenment journey, to dedicate her life's work and purpose to continue on a course of empowering and uplifting others in various ways.

To take a reflective step back, the acknowledgment of the above remained repressed until Monday, August 20, 2012. That day changed her life; forever. After getting off work, driving home, and settling in from the day, she decided to call her husband—who was three hours behind. Upon him answering, she proceeded to engage him in a conversation. In recalling the moment, it could only be described as cold, distant, and abrupt. He did not actually answer any questions posed, and when she attempted to discuss her first visit back to their 'home' in September 2012—he came out with *it* as she started discussing flights; he interrupted her and said, "I want a divorce."

Time froze and the moment was encapsulated in a holding pattern [due to shock]—to say the least. It was as though the pitch of the phone got louder. Everything he said after that, echoed. His speech became more rapid and rushed, and intense. Without knowing what to do or say, she decided that it was best to end the call. As the call ended, emotions flooded her. Fear, anger, agony, shock, and sadness crept in. She began crying. Actually, bawling her eyes out. In an attempt to ascertain why, after crying for over two hours, she texted her husband. She asked him how and why was he doing this? He did not respond. In fact, he did not respond for nearly the next 45 days or so. He refused to speak to her, changed his number, would only communicate with her via email, and became vicious with his words—expressing disdain for her. This was a side of him she had never seen.

Depression and anxiety arose. Depression because of the loss. Anxiety because the plan changed. There was no warning. The plan they had was dependent upon her husband—who would never later join her on the East Coast. After weeks of crying, barely sleeping or eating, and getting up and going to work, showing the world a *fictional face of happiness*, she decided she had to make some choices. Her best option was to remain on the East Coast and return to school—for the fourth time. Why school? Because she would get paid to attend based on her military benefits. Thus, enabling her to have some financial stability in the course of setting up her new, and definitely undesired lifestyle—as she was not able to fully support herself on a single income, even with her full-time position at the time. Upon enrolling in school, she continued to maintain full-time work employment and attended classes in the evenings and on weekends.

Now, fast forward to October 1, 2017. She proudly walked up on stage and was hooded, earning her Doctorate of Education in Counselor Education and Supervision. The thought of the possibility to earn a doctorate was not in the plan of July 28, 2012, when she left the West Coast. However, the nature of the events that lead to her finding happiness and wholeness in herself and her singleness, while working towards professional success, proved: *anything is possible, despite the circumstances and odds.* Now, on the other side of much turmoil, trauma, and tribulations, she is known as Dr. Najah A. Barton or Dr. B.

Reflection:

What circumstances have you experienced, which influence who you are today? How have you positively applied them to propel you into your best self?

Chapter 2

Keep on Living
By Jazmine Blake

July 3, 2016, around 1 in the afternoon, my mom passed away. I'd just left her side. I told her what she needed to hear and what I needed to say. Then, I got in my car and headed home, only to be stopped by a call 10 minutes later saying she had transitioned home. But I didn't cry. I didn't fall apart. I set the ball in motion. I started calling friends and family and letting them know. I started planning and calling for food, ordering flowers and making things happen.

 I sat and laughed and joked with my brother and our friends until I went home, where I didn't sleep. I hadn't slept in weeks. I knew this day was coming, so I tossed and turned and waited for reality to hit after my spiral, my crash. It didn't come. I kept making plans and looking for jobs and continuing life. I had to be strong, for me, my brother, and my late mother. She wouldn't want me to be sad. She would want me to *Keep on Living*; so that's what I did. Until I didn't. I stopped. I stopped living, I simply just existed. I went through the motions. Life was a cycle. I woke up, did things, laid down, and started again. On, the weekends; I pretended to be productive when I just laid around and read or watched shows I'd seen a thousand times. During the week, I was a functioning member of the society who did what I was supposed to. I went to work and pretended to be fine, and then I went home, sat on the couch until I forced myself to go to sleep, where my body did not rest well but just enough to get up and do it again. I was a *robot*. Usually, I did nothing out of my usual routine. Now and then, I'd visit friends and pretend to be 'fine.' Because who wants to hear that I missed my mom so much I couldn't see straight. That taking deep breaths hurt, and doing basic things was nearly impossible. I became what I call, *Functionally Depressed*. I could do just enough each day to seem regular, but once I was away from people, I shut down. My body completely cut off, and even the slightest movements caused immense pain. I didn't shower regularly; I ate anything in reach; I never got off the couch, and I didn't rest when I slept. I was miserable, but I tried to do better.

That first Thanksgiving, I did everything she would have done. We got up and started cooking, we made all the sides (we, as in mostly me), and my brother made dessert. Then when it was time to eat, I was too tired, just like she was. And for a moment, she was with me. Cooking in the kitchen, me sitting on the floor talking to her about all the things at work. I remember her telling me I'm too stubborn and I need to pick my battles. Then for Christmas, I went all out for my nieces and bought all their clothes and things like she did; spending way too much money on everyone so it would seem, normal. December 26 that year, I cried all day. I went back to work and began just functioning again. I cried more now than I think I ever have in my life.

Everything made me cry—driving to work, cooking dinner, hanging out with people, getting invited to events, not getting invited to events, etc. Nothing made me happy. I was a zombie.

It wasn't until our birthdays, my brothers and I, that I started to live again. I wanted our birthdays to be like it was when my mom was still living. I ordered cakes, we had dinner, I tried everything I could remember, but it wasn't the same. I know he enjoyed himself, but I still felt like I could have done more. Then, my birthday came around. First thing in the morning, I slammed my hand in the door before I even left my driveway. Then, I was nearly 30 minutes late to work because of traffic. I hated the day by 8. That is until I walked into work. My teammate had decorated my door; my students brought me cards and sweets. At lunch, my dad and brother showed up with balloons and a birthday cake. I got fruit from my sister-friend and balloons. We had my dinner that night, and I realized *love surrounded me.*

No, my mom wasn't there to guide me, but I still had so many people who even with my recent hermit nature, loved me unconditionally.

I had to change. I started taking care of myself. I was more active (more kitchen runs instead of leaving food on the couch). I spent time with myself and my friends. I found *pieces of myself*. I went to visit my baby brother back home. I met family members that I didn't know existed. I went back to walking more often. I started eating things other than the comfort foods that I could grab and eat anywhere. Fewer biscuits, more apples.

I wasn't running off caffeine and steam anymore; slowly filling in the pieces of the purpose of my life.

In the time since I lost my mother and wrote my story, things have been better, relatively speaking. I'm starting a new business and doing things that I love to do. The one person who defined me, who made me, is watching me and I must make her proud. I continue to struggle with depression, as it is not a "quick fix" situation. I could have easily taken anti-depressants, however, since I rarely remember my allergy pills that help me make it through the day, I decided against pills. It's not easy, but when life goes on as it often does, we must make a conscious effort to make a positive impact for others to follow. I wanted to try exercise as a method of combat. Unfortunately, like many others, my job doesn't end when I get off, and I end up working well into the night; thus keeping exercise from being a viable option. However, I have changed my diet (more salads, fewer biscuits on the couch) and I spend more time with my village (family and friends).

Speaking of my village, I have a select number of people around me whom I keep close to keep me grounded. They are true and dear friends that honestly check on me, not because they want anything, but just because they care. If you are in 'the dark place' and you have people like this, keep them! Don't push them away even when you really, really want to. They will be your light to help you find your way. They may have to help you multiple times; don't feel bad, just support them as well in times of need.

As for my business, *Kissed by Lenore*, it is still a work in progress. Working a full-time job and starting up a business while *battling darkness* is not an easy feat. Because my darkness tends to run things in my life, there are many times where I do not do things as I should. In those times, self-care is not an option. Having recently been in those times frequently and being so far removed from self-care, I am now hyper-focused on making self-care a priority in my community. Nonetheless, in efforts to give back, I host self-care parties and promote self-care tip days via Social Media.

My business is currently based online and is another of those bright spots in my life. I enjoy creating new products for people to take care of themselves. Our line of eczema creams and our latest 'Home Line' are currently my two favorites.

I know my story is not for everyone, but I hope my experience helps someone in their journey with loss and life. May it help you find your way and purpose. Losing my mom was a horrendous loss, but *after death comes living once again*.

Be encouraged to *Keep on Living* amid a great loss, and I am confident that you will be able to live a life full of purpose and destiny. From my heart to yours, *Keep on Living*!

Reflection:

How has this story encouraged you to *Keep on Living*?

CHAPTER 3

THE INSEPARABLE SUSTAINER
BY VANESSA BROWN

Life has been challenging before I even gave birth to my two children. It takes all that is in me to be transparent with people that I do not know, but here it goes. There are many obstacles and struggles that I have experienced during these 42 years. Through mind battles of suicide, depression, oppression, and severe anxiety issues, my children and I stay faithful to God and keep the faith that He will bring us through it all. My babies and I continue to walk this faith walk despite the battles, denials, evictions, repossessions, and the knock-down-drag-out fights.

I teach my children never to lose hope and keep their faith. I also help to plant the seed of God's love in their hearts because love above all will help us to endure life's tests, trials, and challenges. I also remind them that they should always remain humble through the stages of life as they continue to depend on God for His direction. I recall the most challenging of times was for me to maintain a place to stay for my children and reliable transportation. As a result, my children have suffered through the process with me. I am sharing my testimony with you about *The Inseparable Sustainer* to encourage you, not to paint a pity party or for sympathy, but to help you as you go through the process of walking out your purpose. I am honored to have this opportunity to be a *Women of Purpose* Author and share how the anointing of God can destroy every yoke and break every cycle of bondage and defeat! Now, I understand what it means when I hear that *God will take His Children from the back to the front!* He takes His children by the hand and leads us out of despair, confusion, and the wiles of the enemy. It's something when your life is not what you expect it to be, but I still find special ways to sacrifice and bless others. God has given me the heart to bless people whether I know them or not. If I can help someone who expresses a need, I will. I have not always had the resources or positive thoughts, but I have always been transparent with people by sharing my struggles while blessing others in need. Helping others even when I am in the middle of a difficult circumstance is important to me because I am a firm believer that *you reap what you sow.*

I've often verbalized when would my time come to reap the rewards of my sowing so that I could finally walk in my destiny? I am now learning to keep my mouth closed and listen for God's instructions. In the past, I missed many blessings because of my perspective. I also allowed what other people thought about the calling of God on my life to determine my destiny instead of listening to Him for direction. Over time, I have learned; however, to accept people for who they are at face value and walk out my purpose despite them. It was difficult, but the grace of God covered me every step of the way.

To give you a few examples, I've been homeless three times in three years, the same amount of years it took me to complete ministry school. The last bout of homelessness lasted a year and four months, which was by far the hardest to conquer. Regardless of that, *our problems are not our destination!* The generational cycle of physical and emotional abuse in my life had to be healed through a spiritual encounter with God as Jehovah Jireh, *My Provider*. Through a relationship with Him, I've discovered that He is my *Fortress* and *Strong Tower*, and I can depend on Him to always sustain my children and me. When I had no idea how I would make it out of the cycle of abuse that plagued my life, God had orchestrated a master blueprint that drove me right into His *loving arms of provision*. Our Heavenly Father took care of my family, and I am a living witness to tell the story.

Through every experience, disappointment, setback, struggle, mental war, spiritual attack and fight for the integrity of my name, I continued to give God the praise so due to Him.

My ministry is to share my journey from pain to progress in a real way, like the pieces of a puzzle that fit together over time to those who are lost and hurting. God will restore you and reveal *who* you are in the process of elevating you to the position He has for you. Elevation will bring some raw emotions, unchecked voices, and your purpose all at once. That's when you will most likely question yourself and doubt what is happening in your life. Through my experiences, I have learned that God's grace is sufficient to lead and guide us into all truth. *Being unsure is not necessarily a bad thing because it can guide you to seek the face of God.* Upon seeking His guidance, we can positively affect our environment and live the life we want to live. When we trust God and have faith in Him to lead and guide our steps, His promises will come to pass in our lives. However, if we choose to do things our way or to function in the spirit of unbelief with others we know or meet, we set a bad example of His grace.

Believing that He can keep us through the most difficult of times will set us apart as His Beloved. Believe that He is your *Inseparable Sustainer* and walk your purpose out as God shows you what steps to take through faith!

"Now faith is the substance of things hoped for, the evidence of things not seen." (Hebrews 11:1).

Reflection:

How can putting your trust in Jesus possibly change a challenging situation into a positive outcome in your life?

CHAPTER 4

GIRL, BREATHE!
BY VERONICA CLANTON-HIGGINS

"Breathe. Dang it! Breathe!"

I heard a voice…but couldn't open my eyes to see who it was.

"What did she take?!"

I couldn't move. My body felt numb.

"I don't know…I found her like this…"

I couldn't speak. The only thing that I knew is that I wanted to sleep and never wake up!

"We are going to have to pump her stomach!"

I did not want them to pump my stomach. I wanted to be left alone. I wanted to die!

"Look! Do not die on me! Drink this charcoal!"

I closed my mouth tightly and shook my head.

"Drink the charcoal, or we will have to pump your stomach. You do not want us to do that! Drink!"

You see I no longer wanted to be here. I wanted to be free. Free from the emotional turmoil that had risen in my soul because of love; or what I thought was love. You see, I was lying in the back of an ambulance, about to have my stomach pumped because I took some pills. I took pills to help me not be loved anymore. To take away that ache in the core of my spirit. Because if this is what love feels like…I wanted no parts of it. But God had other plans for me. It was not my time to depart from this Earth. I drank the charcoal. A few minutes later, I threw up every single pill that I had swallowed. *Interesting how life is put into perspective when you feel like you are on the verge of losing it.* And I had only been in love for a year.

I had been hiding a secret from family and friends. I was being loved in a dangerous way. This love had infiltrated the depths of my mind and I no longer felt like myself. This love told me what to wear, where to go, took all my money and made me sit in the house and wait for him to return. This love told me that I was nothing and that nobody else would want me. This love threatened to kill itself if I tried to leave. However, *this love was killing me.*

I had allowed myself to believe that love was supposed to be controlling and that to be loved, I had to submit to this treatment. I had been forced to compromise my beliefs to make myself more desirable to him. You see, love informed me that good girls do as they are told and that I was not a good girl. I was not good because I talked back and stood up for myself. But fighting back was my soul's reaction to being mistreated. *I fought to keep a remnant of myself.* In my mind, I knew that I could be a good girl and still be me. This love had locked me in a closet, told me that I was too strong and that I needed to be trained. This love said that *"all women need to be broken!"* This love told me that I thought I was special and it was his job to show me that I wasn't. I remained in this love for seven years. It cost me my sanity, my freedom, my job, and my education.

On September 3, 2003, God sent me an escape. I gave birth to a son. When my son was born, something switched in my brain. I realized that I was no longer responsible for my own life. I had another life to consider. I could not allow my child, to think that love was like this. I left love and found joy—the joy of motherhood. I joined a group of pregnant and new mothers, *Black Infant Health*, who helped me heal my soul, my spirit, and my mind. While in the program, I learned about who I was as a woman and that I deserved to be respected. I discovered the true meaning of love. I now knew that I controlled my destiny and I also set the tone for how I was to be treated. I was able to lay the foundation for the rest of my life.

Finding my strength through motherhood propelled me to *take life by the horns*! I found a job that allowed me the flexibility to be a parent. I enrolled in college. I was living life on my terms! When my son was five months old, I met a wonderful man. He was smart, educated, sensitive, and ambitious. This man showed me what love really is. He loved me for the woman that I am. He loved my son as his own. I eventually became his wife. Shortly after our nuptials, we welcomed a second son. I was experiencing love without fear or restraint.

When I was lying in that ambulance, I was ready for life to be over. My young mind felt that it had experienced everything that it could. I never envisioned the pleasure of being a woman, wife, and mother. To think that if I succumbed to my demons that night, I would not have been able to use my voice to heal others.

You see, through that life lesson, I discovered my resiliency, strength, and determination. I learned that *nothing is impossible*. I finished college, earned a master's degree, started my own business, and I am currently working on my Ph.D. My life became more than being locked in a closet. I was able to take my tragedy and transmute it into triumph.

My tears and my heartache were reflective of the storm I was in. In life, we go through storms, but without storms, we cannot appreciate the rainbows.

So, no matter what you are going through, remember to close your eyes, *breathe*, and enjoy the rainbows. The storm does not last forever.

Reflection:

What time in your life did you feel like giving up but was pushed by a force greater than yourself?

CHAPTER 5

NO PLAN? NO PROBLEM!
BY ALEXANDRIA CUNNINGHAM

*"A man's gift maketh room for him,
and bringeth him before great men."* (Proverbs 18:16).

For many young ladies, the time spent in high school can shape the rest of their lives. High school was not only a highlight of my life but a major turning point as well. Not only did I learn the rigors of academic life, I learned to take risks, step out on faith and be different. My mindset changed. I started believing there was nothing that I could not do. I worked hard academically and physically. I was very involved in extracurricular activities and even held an after-school job.

As my senior year approached, I had no regrets. I saw every situation in my life as a learning experience. Through it all, I had the time of my life. I remember my peers discussing the colleges and universities that had accepted them and how excited they were to shop for their college dorms. It was in those moments a major problem in my life began to arise. My senior year was coming to an end, and I had no plan. I reminded myself of God's Word in Jeremiah 29:11 (NIV), *"For I know the plans I have for you,"* declares the Lord, *"plans to prosper you and not to harm you, plans to give you hope and a future."*

I spent the next few months frantically finding schools to apply to and hoped that I would be accepted. I flipped through a booklet of colleges and universities in my home state, Alabama. I compared class sizes and looked for schools that were not too far from home. I felt as though I had somewhat of an advantage. My dad is a retired *Army Veteran*; this meant that as a dependent, I would be able to attend college with all expenses paid. I would also receive a monthly stipend that gave me the option of quitting my part-time job if I wanted. However, at this point, everything was not all peaches and cream. I had to take the ACT to even be considered for acceptance into a college. I'm not the best test taker in the world. Tests always gave me the worst anxiety.

To make matters worse, I had no idea how to prepare for a test like this. I remember going into the testing room and doing the best that I could. Unfortunately, that test got the best of me! After receiving my test score, I began to review colleges that would consider accepting me based on the ACT score I received. I was accepted to a wonderful HBCU but chose not to go out of fear. It was what I considered too far from home, and that was a priority for me. At that time, I had no transportation or nearby family in case of an emergency. I discovered many of my peers did not have a plan. I then decided to attend a local community college. It wasn't the end of the world. At that point, it was a plan whether others considered it a good one or not.

In May 2009, I began college two weeks after my high school graduation. I was very ambitious and wanted to get ahead. Was I ready for college? Absolutely not! I had no guidance whatsoever. I changed my major quite a few times, wasted a lot of time, money and resources. In life, we're often faced with opposition that leaves our spirit troubled and discouraged. During what seems to be the darkest hour of a person's life, there is a "but God" that turns one's world upside down.

The following year, I began to feel complacent. I was outgrowing my environment and needed *room to grow*. On the way to work one day, my brother's high school sweetheart suggested that I transfer to UWA.

My response to her was, "What's that?"

She laughed and said, "The University of West Alabama in Livingston."

"Where is that?" I asked her.

I had never heard of Livingston in my life. As soon as my shift ended that night at work, I couldn't wait to get home and do some research on this university I have never heard of in a town I had no idea even existed. To my surprise, I discovered that UWA was only 45 minutes from home and the campus was beautiful. I spent the next few days praying and seeking God on what I should do.

I consulted close friends and members of my church about whether I should decide to transfer to the university in Livingston. Selfishly, many of my youth leaders wanted me to stay.

My church brother, Isaiah, sometimes like a godfather to me said, "If you go, you better finish."

Long story short, I weighed my pros and cons. I sought God on the matter daily and began to prepare while I waited for an answer from Him. I developed a strong relationship with the Lord. All in all, my pros outweighed my cons, and the peace of God began to rest upon me.

God will give you peace that surpasses all understanding. Philippians 4:7 says, *"Then you will experience God's peace, which exceeds anything we can understand. His peace will guard your hearts and minds as you live in Christ Jesus."* (NLT).

My gift began to make room for me. I remember going to my counselor to obtain needed documents for my new school. During our conversation, I discovered he once worked as an admissions counselor at UWA. He became one of my mentors within the past year, and I trusted his judgment. He spoke incredibly high of the university.

Shortly after, I saw on social media that my high school color guard instructor would be instructing UWA's color guard during the upcoming fall semester. My instructor was able to secure me a band scholarship without even auditioning. He knew I was good and had four years of experience. At that moment, I began to walk in faith. My mother and I started preparing for my new journey. *God's timing is everything*! Often, I felt as though I missed His calling. I felt as though I turned left when He told me to go right. I rest in knowing that God will never leave nor forsake me (Deuteronomy 31:6b). He goes before me and directs my path.

Moving to Livingston was not easy, especially since I'd never been away from home on my own. There were times where I struggled financially and academically. However, I never lost sight of God and knew that He did not bring me this far just to leave me. I worked numerous jobs on campus, made lifelong relationships and even married my college boyfriend. God took care of me just like He said He would. Sometimes, God wants you to just step out on faith and decide. I'm so glad I did. To this day, I remain in Livingston. It's now home for my husband and me. Living Word Church, also based in Livingston, has instilled the values of love, integrity, faith, and excellence in our lives. I'm glad that after graduating, *I decided to stay and grow.* There's something about this place. Are you facing a situation in your life that requires you to *turn up your faith*? You may feel as though you are at a crossroad, deciding on which path to take. Discover your gifts and give them back to

God's kingdom for His glory. My gift made room for me, and your gift can make room for you too!

Reflection:

Do you know what your spiritual gift or gifts are? To find out go to www.smarturl.it/spiritualgifts.

CHAPTER 6

THIS WAS IT!
BY NIKEISHA DARENSBURG

This was it! I slowly exhaled as I placed the plain business letter envelope on the kitchen countertop. I didn't want to leave like this, but based on history; I knew if I tried to leave while he was home, it would be met with resistance. Argue, fight, makeup, repeat. It was time to break the vicious cycle that for the past seven years, masqueraded itself as love. It was time to walk away from the toxicity that left me feeling increasingly devalued and defeated inside. Time to walk away from the helplessness and hopelessness that sought to exalt itself over my purpose and passion.

As I stood in the living room, I took one last look around and mentally said my goodbyes. It wasn't *all* bad. I looked at the chocolate sofa, now sans decorative pillows, and thought about the countless times he and I had curled up to watch movies, complete with movie theatre butter popcorn and candy. Twizzlers for him, M&M's with peanuts for me. I allowed my eyes to roam to the space once occupied by my desk. The desk where I'd spent hours working on one school paper, after another, after another. He'd come up behind me and massage my shoulders and ask if I needed help with anything. He would bring me something to drink and put it next to my laptop as I continued to be lost in thought. Typing away furiously, engrossed in my latest project.

I walked over to the kitchen and relived all the nights when he'd be standing at the kitchen sink, washing dishes with his headphones on and looking out the window; a man that would voluntarily cook and wash the dishes. Each step I took brought back another memory. I remembered how he'd taken care of me when I was sick. He would care for me with so much compassion, refusing to let me do anything except getting well and going to the restroom. I smiled at the thought.

My breathing became shallow as I fought back the tears. Maybe I was making a mistake...Did I really want to throw seven years down the drain? I thought I was doing what I needed to do, but now I wasn't so sure. I loved this man. I love this man. I felt as though my heart was beating out of my chest. I lost the battle to contain my tears. Before I knew it, I was crying an ugly cry. Gasping, I felt as though the air was trying to suffocate me as I struggled to breathe. I gripped the wall as I slid down to the floor.

My head rested on my knees, and I sought to gather my composure. Deep breaths. I inhaled slowly, exhaled even slower. I did this until I was able to breathe easily again. I got up to use the bathroom when something sharp stabbed me in the bottom of my foot. Wincing in pain, I looked at my bloodied heel and saw a piece of glass stuck in my foot. It was then that I noticed the broken glass on the floor. I walked into the bedroom that we shared and saw a bottle of *Johnny Walker Red* next to the bed. He was drinking again. He was an angry drunk. Suspicious, destructive, and unpredictable. My fond memories and any doubts about my decision to leave were quickly replaced with harsh reminders of how I'd gotten to this point. We had some of the worst arguments I'd ever experienced in my life. He said it was because we were so passionate about one another. I recognized it to be *cohesive dysfunction*. We'd been having different versions of the same arguments for seven years. Seven years of name calling, door slamming, object throwing, going for days without speaking, accusations…insinuations.

Argue, fight, makeup, repeat. After a while, it takes its toll. I was tired. Mentally exhausted, soul interrupted. At one point, I thought that if I didn't say anything back, didn't engage in the arguments; they'd cease. It takes two to argue they said. Obviously, *they* didn't know him. I found myself getting angry again as I recalled our fight two weeks ago. I couldn't remember what it was about, but I did recall refusing to allow myself to get sucked into his rabbit hole. As he continued to glare at me and yell across the room, my body was there, but my mind was someplace far away. Any attempts at dissolution and peace only seemed to infuriate him further. My efforts to leave were futile, as his physical strength overpowered mine and he barricaded the door.

That night, as I laid there with my back turned towards him, I began to cry myself to sleep. I tried to mask my angst under the *shield of darkness*, but my stifled sobs betrayed me. He pulled me into his embrace and sought to console me, apologized over and over, as he smoothed my hair and kissed my face.

He repeatedly professed his love for me, which made me cry even harder. I cried because I believed him. I cried because while he loved me with every fiber of his being, he still couldn't love me the way that I needed to be loved. The way I deserved to be loved. See, I was taught that there is no fear in love. *Love is supposed to drive out fear, not incite it.*

I knew what I had to do. As I loaded the last container on the U-Haul truck and drove away, peace came over me. I smiled, thankful for the lessons. Never again would I transmute my identity or condense my essence to fit inside anyone else's box.

This was the day that I decided to starve my fears and binge on my faith. This was the day I decided to demonstrate to my daughters that it was okay to still love someone yet love yourself enough to walk away.

This was it.

Proverbs 19:21 says, *"Many are the plans in a person's heart, but it is the LORD'S purpose that prevails."*

Nothing could be more profound as it applies to my life. My previous experiences with my (then) boyfriend have shown me that God's gift and calling are truly irrevocable. I've known for some time that my purpose is to reach women who have been through similar situations, single mothers, and those with insecurities. However, like Jonah, I tried to run away from my calling because it made me uncomfortable. Instead, I sought solace in a relationship that was toxic and that I should not have been in. No matter how bad things got, I fought to hold on to the very thing that God was trying to tear me away from.

Because of my insecurities and fear, I allowed my relationship to overshadow my life and ambition. God allowed me to go through some ordeals that led me to finally say, 'Enough is enough.' *This Was It* chronicles the beginning of an end for me. Where I finally decided to let go of my fear and step out on faith. That was the point in my life where I decided to live in total transparency and share my ugly truth.

Women go through so much behind closed doors, and we often smile… wear a mask of sorts and pretend that everything is okay. Meanwhile, on the inside, we're wasting away, depending on a man, when we should be leaning on God. By walking in truth and sharing my story, my experience has given me the boldness to write my upcoming novel, *Torn*.

In addition to my novel, I am in the process of creating a group that is geared primarily towards single women and young mothers. The focus of this group will help them to recognize their purpose, achieve the skills and social supports that they need, and to achieve financial independence as well as foster their well-being.

Reflection:

When some people think of self-love, they think it's synonymous with being selfish. What were your views on self-love before reading my story? Did your perspective change?

CHAPTER 7

FINDING THE STRENGTH
BY BENTA DAVIS

I truly believe that words are the most powerful tools in life. They have the power to uplift and the power to tear down. It's important to understand the way we decide to use our words when speaking to other people. I realized at an age when I was vulnerable to the judgments around me how detrimental words and language could be. To recognize the power of language and social interaction is to really understand how to appreciate people. Have you ever been told you can't do something? The power of these words can drastically change a person's life to the point where they can believe that no matter what, nothing in their life can or will change.

I used to think that there were limits and rules to what I could carry out, that life was like that. I believed the negativity; words like *stupid* that tear down the belief that a person could ever amount to anything, that you could never be good enough, be accomplished enough or work hard enough to get anywhere. Words like ugly that can outcast, isolate, and unnecessarily place value on image and appearance. Words like these change the way we think and navigate through the world and affect us mentally, physically and emotionally.

I was never the smartest student, not the prettiest or the most social. I was insecure, self-conscious, and overweight in my younger years. *I did not like me.* I cared a lot about what other people thought of me and became increasingly burdened by image and appearance. I never thought I could lose weight and I remember giving up. I remember saying to myself; I don't care how I look anymore, this is it, and there is nothing that I can do about it. I tried and failed, and that was that! I remember crying in the mirror convinced that nothing would change, that I couldn't change. I was hung up with the idea that I would be more likable, that my life would be better if I could just lose weight. These ideas made me sad and self-conscious to the point where I hid my emotions so that nobody could see my real feelings. Until one day, I had enough with the self-pity. I could no longer feel sympathy for my situation, and I was tired of giving up. I was angry at myself for not trying and letting myself get to such a low point. I stood in the mirror looking at my reflection, and I finally said the words that I needed to hear.

You can do it, Benta, *you* can do this! Words are powerful. When I said those words, I felt them! At that moment, I was ready to lose weight. *I made a decision, and I was not going back*! It was time to make a change, and I was ready to commit to losing the weight, a burden I carried with me for most of my life. I was ready to let it go, and I was doing it for me and my health. I began educating myself about the food that I was putting into my body. I spoke with a nutritionist about healthy eating, and she showed me a lifestyle that promoted a balanced diet and regular exercise. Slowly but surely, I started losing weight. I began to feel more confident and outgoing as the scale dropped from 225, 190, 170 to 140 pounds. I continued to motivate myself with positivity and words of encouragement and my friends and family supported my journey as well. As I reached my weight loss goal, I believed more than ever that I could truly do anything. My weight loss was a huge challenge for me, and I never thought that I would be able to overcome it, but I did. In the process, I grew into a stronger person. I now truly believe I can do anything, no matter what anyone else says and no matter what anyone thinks. My strength and determination can never be taken away from me.

"It takes a lot of courage to be able to look past what people say and think to really see the person you are inside especially when you don't fit the mold, or you feel that you don't belong."

I look back at and remember who I was and how I have changed and the people who have encouraged me to take chances. I am now able to look past fear and not be afraid to act in pursuit of my goals and dreams. I used their guidance, and in the process, I have been able to inspire others of all ages to take chances, to challenge themselves to dream bigger, and set higher goals.

Since my weight loss, I've gained the confidence to take chances and experience the world. I have been able to step outside of my comfort zone and live and work abroad in Spain and Burkina Faso as a Teacher. I'm blessed to have a chance to teach and give back to my community and different people around the world. To teach young people, especially young women to believe in themselves, to be confident and to take chances, and to give back to their communities by sharing their own experiences.

My weight loss journey gave me the confidence to be able to encourage others to believe that no goal is unreachable.

Reflection:

What challenges are you dealing with today that you can decide right now to face head-on and conquer?

CHAPTER 8

LIFE IN WORDS
BY JUDY DAVIS

Until my daughter approached me about this chapter, the writing of one's life's events, I had never given thought to how certain events, places, and people have affected the different directions of my six decades and four years of life. All praises I give to God with tears of joy! Born of seventeen children, to Nelson Davis and Sallie Moore in Wilson County, North Carolina in 1954; we were a sharecropper family. My mother; was a hard-working woman and a provider for our family. She was faced with the decision to leave the farm and my father.

In her own words, she said, "I couldn't take it any longer!"

When she left, she shocked everyone while taking my baby sister with her as she headed to Washington, D.C. I was eight years old when my mother left. I was sad and hurt, but I knew she would be back for us like she said she would.

My mother came back just as she said, and we headed to Washington, leaving the farm and North Carolina. Being a woman from the South, when we moved to Washington, my mother was very overprotective and strict, especially with her five younger children. I was not allowed to go far from home, and I stayed near the front porch of our house with the younger children until I was eighteen and old enough to venture outside of the neighborhood where I would soon meet a young man. He was a little older than me and had been making eyes at me over the years up until my senior year. On the night of my eighteenth birthday, I ventured out to meet him, and one thing led to another. Little did I know this was just the beginning of the first major event of my life. The next week, I visited the neighborhood doctor to get birth control pills. I remember the smirk on the doctor's face as he handed me a business card with the name of an abortionist. This was his way of telling me that I was pregnant. As I think back, it was like yesterday. I was so close to graduating in three months and taking a class trip. But now, I felt very lost and alone and afraid. I did not want my mother to know. I decided I did not want to have a baby. I did not think I was ready to be a mother. What did I know? I never told my mother or anybody about my abortion, but I felt she knew but never said anything. *I vowed never to do that again.*

A year later, I started attending the University of District of Columbia for engineering, only to drop out to make more money working for the U.S. Postal Service.

Before leaving UDC, I went on a camping trip that would change my life. Veterans from the University sponsored the trip. They took a group of us out, and we learned about camping. On our trip, they taught us about food and showed us how to grill on an open fire. We made Sloppy Joe's that looked and tasted so good. The Veterans educated us on how to eat and live without killing animals. They told us things about how meat turned to maggots in the body. After the trip, I did not want to eat meat anymore and decided to stop eating meat for good. Since then, I've never eaten meat again, and in the last ten years, I have changed to a completely vegan diet with 60% raw whole foods. While working at the Post Office, I was an excellent worker, and my supervisor promoted me to a full-time position. During my employment, I met the father of my now five beautiful daughters and four handsome boys, and I give God the praise for my family.

Years later, while pregnant with our first child and living a completely vegetarian lifestyle, I was introduced to a natural foods store, Glut Food Co-Op, where I started shopping. The smell of the store, the herbs and spices would make me nauseous being pregnant at the time. I could not stay in the store long. Once I had the baby, I had no problems and started volunteering regularly. Volunteering was a great way to make food credit to spend in the store and help with my new lifestyle. My work performance was always very good, and I was asked if I wanted to work in the store full-time since a place had opened. I said yes! It has now been 37 years since the birth of my first child and my start at Glut Food Co-Op. 37 years later, my children are grown, and I am a grandmother to six wonderful grandchildren. I am not very wealthy with money. I have my family and my health. *After all, what is money if you don't have your health and family to share it with?* Health is wealth.

Reflection:

Do you value money, position or power over your health and happiness?

CHAPTER 9

OVERCOMING ABUSE
BY CHONTAE EDISON

I remember it like it was yesterday. On that day, we talked on the phone, and he said he would come over a little later. The moment I heard the doorbell, I hurriedly ran to open the door. I was so excited to see him. We greeted each other with a hug and headed toward my room. Once we sat down on the bed, I felt a sudden burning sensation on the side of my face. My cheek was on fire! *He had slapped me.* Tears began to fill my eyes and run down my face in an instant. I was in utter disbelief.

What is going on? Did I do something wrong? I'm so sorry for whatever it is I may have done. I thought to myself.

At that moment, for some odd reason, I didn't feel worthy. I ran to the bathroom and grabbed a handful of medicine. I counted out roughly ten Advil pills and proceeded to swallow. All I wanted was for the pain to stop and the hurt to go away. I longed for peace and happiness to replace my misery. I couldn't understand why this was happening to me. This man came into my life during a time when I had everything going for me. I had friends, a good job, and a great life. He turned my life upside down. My so-called great life wasn't so great anymore. Now, I was in an abusive relationship. I was hopeless, broken, sad, lonely, and suicidal. I felt like I had no way out.

This was my life almost 12 years ago. While I quickly realized I needed to get out of that relationship, the other lingering issues weren't so easy for me to fix. It was hard for me to address my issues of self-worth, insecurities, and loneliness.

Asking myself, "How do I rebuild my life from this point?" Always questioning my worth. During that period in my life, those were the thoughts I had running through my head until I realized *the power resides in me.*

The word *"power"* has various definitions, but the most appropriate definition that I identify with is the ability to act or produce an effect. I began to realize the only way I could create change would be to start with myself and find *power* from within.

One of the first steps I took was writing out a list of my goals. I decided to go back to school and obtain my bachelor's degree. At first, I struggled in the beginning while trying to juggle the cost of school, time management, and my full-time job. Fortunately, I managed to find applicable resources and save money. After a year of going to school part-time, I decided to become a full-time student. Before I knew it, I was in a position where I didn't have to take out student loans to cover the cost. I graduated college in three and a half years, and my $30,000 tuition was paid in full.

My next goals were to move out of state, find a job, and get my own place. During this transition, I saved my money and paid off my car. That allowed me to lower my expenses in preparation for my big move. Six months later, I moved into an apartment and found a job shortly after.

While all of this was happening, I noticed a pattern and a change of emotion with every achievement. I began to feel empowered, strong, independent, confident and certain.

Four years later, a new opportunity presented itself, and I became a homeowner. However, my life did not come full circle until one evening I was sitting at home and decided to start a blog. That is when iheartbrowngirl.com was born.

On so many occasions, we as women, especially brown women, can reach out and touch one another but we don't. This blog represents my experiences and others who are willing to share thought-provoking topics that most women are afraid to talk about with their mate, family, or friends.

My story is the story of so many other women. I choose to share my story because I want other women to know that you too can overcome any obstacle. While my situation may not be to the extent of others, I was able to overcome the physical, emotional, and mental abuse of my past amongst many other obstacles.

My whole outlook on life has changed because of the obstacles I had to overcome, and I began to realize that I had the *power* all along. I worked on myself to become the best me I could be. I had to stop being the victim and take control over my life. Thanks to therapy, great friends, and family, I was able to move forward in my life. *The key is being open to change.*

So many times, I wanted to cry, and I did. Life was hard. The feelings I described to you at the beginning of this story would occasionally resurface, but as time passed, I became stronger and better. I love me. I love who I have become, and I respect me! I want all women to realize they too have the *power*. Too many times, we give our power away so quickly or too easily. The *power* starts with you!

I encourage every woman reading this to reflect on their journey and learn from it. We have so many opportunities to be the best version of ourselves, but we somehow lose our power and strength in someone else or life. Life happens, but remember you are not alone on this journey and you are capable!

Reflection:

In what area of your life have you relinquished your power to someone else that you can now take back?

Chapter 10

Making a Statement for Love
By Rashell Evans

Sometimes, life reveals the answer to a question you didn't realize you were asking. When I think about walking in my purpose, I do not think about the woman who sits here writing this piece today. Rather, I think about a specific moment in time, years ago, near a campfire in upstate New York. A couple of my friends and I decided to go camping to bond with each other under the stars, alongside wildlife. That evening, we set up a campfire and started sharing stories about the work week, when someone suggested we take turns expressing how much we truly adored one another. This went on for what felt like hours and the night bellowed with laughter, tears, a few hugs and genuine sisterhood.

The weekend commenced with one adventure after another until it was time to find a Starbucks and head home. The entire ride home, I felt like a fraud. The night before, by the campfire, I learned that my closest friends, my sisters, thought that I was brave and fearless. Little did they know, it was the furthest thing from the truth. I didn't make a deliberate decision to be fearless, outspoken, and resilient. See, by the time I was a pre-teen, I'd experienced a lot of losses over the years, including that of my parents. I'm just a brown girl from the Bronx who lived with her maternal grandmother and as an only child; my motto in life quickly became 'me, myself, and I.' My outlet was writing and reading books. I'd get lost in the pages of books and escape the feelings I couldn't express in my writing—that was my therapy. After my mother passed away, I went to see a counselor on a single occasion, and she essentially told me that I'd be lucky if I didn't become a statistic. I don't think there was a single epiphany or moment of realization that I could no longer escape within the pages of books. Anger and fear took over. I'd experienced huge trauma surrounding the loss of my mother. By the time I was a young adult, I believed I wasn't allowed to continue feeling the hurt from my loss. I bottled it up, and it manifested itself in a quest to disconnect and never lose anyone again.

What others saw as fearless was really a young woman in pain; someone determined not to care about anyone, but herself. The first chance I got, I left home and attended the first HBCU, Lincoln University. Graduated with honors and continued my education at Baruch College in New York City, where I received my master's degree. During my college career, societal norms, and my ego developed a checklist of goals I was supposed to accomplish in the name of being a "good" black woman. By the time I was 24 years old, I'd accomplished all but three of those goals. Career job, multiple degrees, homeownership, car, money in my savings and checking account; the list went on.

Can you believe at the end of it all, I was still *unhappy*? There was no parade at the end of my checklist. Where were my banners and the marching band led by the counselor who told me I'd be lucky if I weren't a statistic? I had to accept that no one was there because I'd pushed everyone away. I wasn't fearless and brave for being outspoken when it was time to accomplish another goal or leaving home with no money to pursue college. Unbeknownst to me, I was a just a hurt and scared woman who didn't allow herself to be transparent with anyone, just so she could prove to everyone that she was *good enough*.

The day I began walking in my purpose was the day I decided to open my heart and let love in. This was not an easy thing for me to do. *My advice to women includes finding a professional therapist to speak with*. There's a stigma within the black community when it comes to therapy. I too bought into the stigma once upon a time, but mental health is a part of your overall health. Seeking professional advisement comes with a level of vulnerability, trust, transparency, and most importantly, self-awareness.

Daily, I use a little less logic and allow my heart to lead from time to time. These days, my motto is no longer 'me, myself and I.' However, I live by the golden rule that 'what doesn't work is information.' I can live with that.

Today, I am truly fearless and brave. My purpose is to mentor and activate young women to be great in whichever lane they choose. In 2017, I founded Statement Junky, a non-profit organization dedicated to gifting girls with the essential key to access the world—their first passport.

In conjunction with the tangible passport, our online media pages and website, *StatementJunky.com* is designed to inform, empower, and inspire girls to explore the world. I started Statement Junky because there is knowledge and power in having a global perspective as a girl. Our girls are bombarded daily with images and storylines dictating the girl they're supposed to be.

By reaching beyond the borders of her community, girls and young women all over the nation, with a passport in hand, can explore the world and in turn change the world. Travel fosters empathy and a commitment to community and service. The greatest gift is when a mentee expresses an interest in paying it forward, to mentor others on the importance of travel.

Our future depends on a new breed of leaders, ready to solve the world's problems. Passion will only take one so far. Leaders need the right mix of values, skills, and worldly experiences to fulfill their purpose.

Reflection:

If travel is a key to education, how far does a girl have to travel to change the world?

Chapter 11

Marathon Runner
By Incredible Faith

"But the one who stands firm to the end will be saved."
(Matthew 24:13).

Life is a *marathon*, never a race. Oftentimes, we begin new ideas, new jobs, and new relationships with an unlimited amount of energy, optimism, faith, and excitement. We hear a word from God and believe for that moment that anything is possible. On our knees, we pray and create an atmosphere of worship. We write the vision, we meditate, and we ask God for His will to be done. Then, just as a sprinter assumes the start position of a race, so do we, as we stand up onto our feet. However, what if I told you that most things in life are not a race but rather a *marathon*? Would you be able to create the same energy needed to maintain adequate endurance for the task? Or will you burn out, once you realize that not every day can be a sprint?

It's almost like deciding never to eat meat again, and you have never gone a day in your life without it. On day 1, you are committed, motivated, and faithful. By day 5, you can barely hold on, your energy is low, your attitude begins to shift negatively, and you are no longer enacting in your new task with a positive mind and pure heart.

Quite honestly, I have had difficulty numerous times in maintaining an adequate level of commitment, faith, balance, and endurance in my life. Reflecting on the process, it was the knowledge of Christ and His authority in my life that kept me grounded and focused.

"*I can do all this through Him who gives me strength.*" (Philippians 4:13).

After graduating from the illustrious *Spelman College*, I was able to meet many new friends within the entertainment industry, and being in L.A., it was such a pleasure, an outlet from the conservative approach my daily activities provided. Being creative at heart, I decided to set my eyes on a path to become a Grammy Award Winning Artist. Without much confirmation from God, I began to engage in outrageous business deals because *I was thirsty to get my cup filled!* Heck, I was sprinting in a marathon! Unfortunately, this led me to lose large sums of money, many friends, and quite a few failed business attempts and ideas.

My mindset, passion, and overall vision began to fizzle and slowly burn out. My endurance was no longer able to provide the strength I needed to finish each day of my marathon. How many times do we hear of our families', colleagues', friends', or loved ones' success, but question God and ourselves on the deliverance of our own? Again, if life is a marathon, how often do we slow our pace or even step into the wrong lane to chase something that we were neither designated nor built to run in? We become burnt out; we question our life, our existence, *we even lose track of our purpose*, all the while trying to obtain something that may or may not be our true calling. I had to let impatience, envy, pride, stubbornness, regret, shame, '*title of your fleshly struggle here,*' go...

I had to pour my heart out unto God for *healing*, direction, and guidance. It was in those moments, wet and clammy cheeks, snotty nose, prayer affirmations coated with spit, that I found God, my passion and purpose.

Hebrews Chapter 12:1 – *"Therefore, since we are surrounded by such a great cloud of witnesses, let us throw off everything that hinders and the sin that so easily entangles. And let us run with perseverance the race marked out for us."*

Many of us are dream-chasers, leaders, lovers, courageous, strong, and independent women. My question is, why are we ashamed to believe and receive what God has for us? More importantly, once we believe and receive, why do we go full throttle instead of allowing God to control our speed? No matter your marathon, you must be able to obtain a positive and peaceful mindset while in route to your ordained prosperity. One way to ensure you remain balanced, consistent, and focused during a marathon is having the word of God to fall back on, for it is surely the nourishment of our mind, body, and soul.

Isaiah Chapter 40:31 – *"But those who hope in the Lord will renew their strength. They will soar on wings like eagles; they will run and not grow weary, they will walk and not be faint."*

Did I fail at my first attempt at becoming the Whitney Houston of *Gospel Rap*? You bet! But that was never God's intended purpose.

Instead, He anointed me to write, create, lead, and love through by combining my creative and business acumen to educate, empower, and encourage millennials, minorities, and women just like you to find their true calling.

While reading this, you will come to envision in your mind an area in your life where you have either burned out, failed or given up due to a lack of endurance or a tainted heart. My prayer for you is that you decide to meditate on the scriptures within this chapter and go back to your initial reason for beginning, and start again.

May the Lord open your heart to the ability to heal your brokenness and may the Prince of Peace reign over your mind to comfort and strengthen you, knowing that you can and will succeed, as you are the seed of a strong and mighty King who will help you keep the pace and win the race.

> *"Do you not know that in a race all the runners run,*
> *but only one gets the prize?*
> *Run in such a way as to get the prize."*
> (1 Corinthians 9:24).

Nothing's left. Hold your breath.
Don't you dare get full of regret!
You done did it now. Don't frown.
Don't drop your head and lose your crown.
We all make mistakes,
have the strength to get back up again.
You can win. It all comes from within.
Call on Him!

Yes, there's work you have to do.
Don't worry He will guide you.
Have faith! He won't mislead you.
Let your pain, be the reason.
Let your depression be what you use,
to do what you must do, need to do.
With the faith the size of a mustard seed,
you can move any mountain…
So young believer, why the heavy feet?
"Well, I'm stuck and idk how I got myself here!"
"Chase a check or chase my purpose?"

"Hesitation got not only my feet but my heart heavy."
But unlike them Levis,
I won't let any Hurricane,
flood emotions all over my face.
Slowly learning it's not about how fast you run,
but how you finish the race.

No matter how many practices you put in place,
it won't stop you from running,
at your own natural pace.
Meaning the longer you mimic another runner's race,
the longer you make your own race.
Maybe you need some time to reflect and meditate.
Then you may be able to relate.
Should you fall, don't choose to let the pain,
harden your heart & you begin to player hate.

Why?
What does their success have to do with your race?
Since you are looking down,
go ahead and tie your shoelace.
Look up and thank God for His mercy & grace.
Marathon runner, are you ready?
Pow! Pow!
Start your race.

It's never too late to begin a marathon, and it's never too soon to change your pace back to the tempo God created for your life. Young sister, Christ is within you and in all you do, please know with Him you cannot fail!

Acts Chapter 20:24 – *"However, I consider my life worth nothing to me; my only aim is to finish the race and complete the task the Lord Jesus has given me – the task of testifying to the good news of God's grace."*

Love, Light and Life, *Incredible Faith*.

Reflection:

What task is set before you to finish your race?

CHAPTER 12

A Leap from Fear toward Purpose
By Nealy Gihan

As a kid, I was afraid of everything, especially thunder and lightning! Each time there was a storm, I remember closing my eyes tightly and making my ears sore by shoving my fingers in them to shut out the noise. If I couldn't see nor hear the storm, I figured, just maybe there'd be nothing to fear. Growing up, I avoided any and everything I was afraid of, and it prevented me from doing a lot. I never told the guy in high school I was crushing on that I liked him because I was afraid he wouldn't like me back. Right after college, I didn't take a dream job in Puerto Rico because I was afraid of living so far away from home. I used to let fear keep me from fulfilling my purpose.

There's this mantra I learned in college about fear. I'm not sure if someone paraphrased it from the popular Sci-Fi series *Dune* or if it came before the books. What I do know is that it's something I can still recite as easily as John 3:16 or the theme song to *The Fresh Prince of Bel-Air*. Yet, I never really thought about the words nor gave them any validity until the day I stood trembling atop a platform in the trees dozens of feet above the ground in Panama.

"Fear is a mind killer. It is a little evil that disintegrates me from the inside out. I must learn to face it and control it. Fear."

That day in the rainforest of El Valle de Anton, in my mid-twenties, I was absolutely terrified of more than just falling to my death. I was also afraid of the life awaiting me back home in Illinois and what my future held. Regardless of every fiber in my body telling me to turn and run away from my fears like always, however, I mumbled that mantra under my breath, leaped off the platform toward my fears, and ziplined through a canopy of lush greenery, toucans, and waterfalls. That exhilarating experience was my ever-important first step of courage that has propelled me down the long, winding, yet steady path toward becoming a published author and entrepreneur.

I'd come to Panama despondent and fearful, but in this life-changing moment, I learned to face these emotions and conquer them. First, I'd flirted with the idea of doing a Spanish immersion program in Panama a year before I went.

"Wouldn't it be so cool?"

I remember asking my parents the Saturday morning after I'd gotten literature on the program. Like a child, I'd climbed into bed with my folks and snuggled between them with the papers. But I knew I'd never do it. It was too scary, and I was comfortable in my suburban life, job, and graduate school.

Then the unimaginable happened. After decades of marriage, my parents were getting a divorce. My dad was moving out and leaving us. I began to fear my dad didn't love me enough to stay, that no one would ever love me enough. I would never be good enough nor at anything. My thoughts and fears of abandonment, rejection, and inadequacy consumed me and spiraled away from the rational. Fear is a liar. It is a mind killer.

Suddenly, home was scarier than being in a foreign country thousands of miles away from where I poorly spoke the language.

So, I escaped to Panama. The funny thing is, all those insecurities came right with me.

I learned that suppressing your feelings, especially fear, solves nothing. There's nothing wrong with feeling afraid or insecure. The problem occurs when you become your emotions and give in to fear. To take control, you have to acknowledge where fear comes from.

It's not of God. The Bible states that God has not given us a spirit of fear. In 2 Timothy 1:7, it states: *"For the Spirit God gave us does not make us timid, but gives us power, love, and self-discipline."* (NIV).

Fear comes from the enemy. It is his most popular weapon used to parallelize us and keep us from the goodness and purposes God has for us. This is why God tells us in the Bible so many times not to be afraid. He recognizes that it is our natural inclination to be afraid, but in Him, we don't have to be. Although I ran to Panama afraid, trying to escape, God had other plans for me there. I fell in love with the country—the Bird of Paradise flowers that grew wild along the roadside, the sloths hanging free from the trees, the dolphins that swam peacefully around our boat in the water, my loving host family, and the sky accented by the most colorful birds and butterflies. I saw God in everything! It all reminded me just how good He is and how much bigger He is than any fear I could have. I remembered that God is for me, with me, and in control. He does not just tell us in the Bible not to be afraid; He also promises to never leave us, to strengthen us, to help us, to keep us safe, and to give us a future beyond our fears. We only have to believe and trust in Him. (John 3:16).

That's what led me to stand in a tree some thirty feet above the ground with the courage to jump. I was still afraid, but I believed in a God who was bigger than my fear of heights and everything else. At that moment, I chose to no longer let my mind-killing, destructive fears control me. I chose to focus on what was true, instead of the irrational thoughts that had taken hold of me. I decided not to allow fear to paralyze me from living a full and purposeful life. I took the leap, screaming and terrified the whole time. Fear no longer controlled my mind!

Today, years later along the journey, I admit, I still get scared. With every story I write, I fear no one will read it, or everyone will and hate it. I fear my editing and copywriting business, Purple Inked, will fail. Yet, I continue writing and investing in my business anyway. *I jumped from trees in Panama and lived triumphantly*. With God in my life, I've learned how to face my fears, control them, and go forward in my purpose and so can you!

Reflection:

Name a fear holding you back from reaching your potential. Is it rational? How do God's promises contradict your fear?

CHAPTER 13

GETTING MY LOVE IN ORDER
BY DR. SANDRA HAMILTON (HILL)

It is said, *"What does not kill you will make you stronger,"* and it seems that the philosopher, Friedrich Nietzsche, was indeed right. One ordinary Thursday evening in August 2015, on my way home from work, I was hit head-on by a truck, whose driver was not paying attention. I experienced unusual strength and learned from that near-death experience.

I saw this big metal square that had Suburban written on it (A big Suburban SUV truck was heading straight to me at 67 mph). I recalled slamming both feet on the floor of my vehicle and stiffly bracing myself with my two arms on the steering wheel for the hit. The first hit to my vehicle seemed to lift my vehicle off the ground, and I felt it spin (in very slow motion) with about a 270-degree turn, then I recalled letting go of the wheel and saying in a very calm voice, *"Today is the end of my life."* I thought of my family, and my children having to come and identify my body there. I then remembered shortly after that thought, saying, "Thank you, Lord, for giving me all this time here on earth."

Suddenly, I felt my vehicle make a big drop as it crash-landed...and everything else became a big fog.

I woke up in torturous traction in the hospital in a lot of pain—neck, arms, legs, and body, locked down on a board, not allowed to move. Albeit, I had a strange sense of calmness and peace enveloping me in the midst of it all. The Suburban landed on top of my vehicle. My windshield broke, all airbags exploded, and I sustained many burns. The expanding airbag hit my face. My nose had a hairline fracture. Both front airbags were triggered by the frontal crash. I had a temporary unilateral hearing loss. The chemical from the airbags etched my facial skin. My chest, sternum, and arms were bruised, and I had contusions on my legs. I also lost a portion of my left shin, had whiplash, damage to my cervical spine and shoulders. My entire body was seriously injured. I experienced shortness of breath for several months, anxiety and stress plagued me. I was unable to sleep and rest as previous and could not enjoy quality time any longer. Life for me as it were, changed in the *twinkling of an eye*! For approximately twenty months, my new norm became chronic, throbbing pain, yet God was saying to me, "There is more that I require of you..."

I could not give up, would not give up, knowing there was so much more purpose for me to complete. So, I continued to press on, working as hard as possible as a disabled person in every area of my life.

An invisible blanket of warmth enveloped me continuously, throughout the chronic injuries. It was a luminous, very warm but not burning type of heat. I could not tell exactly what it was. I will spare you all the details of the whole thing, but I got two prayers granted: that day, that I would not die there, and that my family would not have to identify my body amid the horrendous wreck.

Two officers surrendered their lives to Christ that day once they saw me at the hospital, based on the glow they said that I had.

They said, "Whatever you have, I want that too."

GETTING MY LOVE IN ORDER

I had cracked ribs and a serious concussion. I felt like I was shipwrecked and coming back to the shoreline on thousands of tiny broken pieces. The presence the officers saw on me, to this day, I now know was the Comforter, God's Holy Spirit, covering me.

My insurance company insisted that someone in charge of my vehicle, release it to them. On my way home, after being discharged from the hospital, I was taken to see my vehicle. The closer I got, the more curious I became and even got goosebumps.

The tow yard manager met us at the gate and said, "You must be the driver's family members, I am so sorry for your loss."

He then remained in shock, realizing I was the driver. Part of the roof of my vehicle had been crushed into the back seat. And other parts of the roof had been crushed on the driver side as well!

I guess you could say that I, a well-educated, thought to be an accomplished woman, one who said she was a fantastic driver at that, looked at this totaled pile of metal, and knew she had so much to be thankful for! And so much more to do in the world, with so little time, as I cried tears of gratefulness to God for saving my life and giving me 'a little more time.'

Everything in life happens for a reason. That is why being hit head-on in the collision that day, changed my life forever. It caused me to turn from worshipping worthless 'stuff' to elevating my discipline to treasure God, at a whole new level. The near-death experience instilled the reality that life is 'but a vapor,' 'temporary,' yet God carefully plans it out before we are born.

Jeremiah 1:5 says, *"Before I formed you in the womb, I knew you."*

What an amazing thought: God knew me before I was even born! He saw my unformed substance and said that He had a purpose for my life. It seemed crazy but, I found confidence in God's love for me, amid a deadly car accident, knowing that He orchestrated my existence before the beginning of time! Therefore, nothing could stop my purpose, not a head-on collision, not pain, injury, brokenness, absolutely nothing! I just had to stay focused, and not give up.

I got a chance to get my love in the right order. And that I did! A second chance to get serious about accomplishing my God-given purpose, and I have not stopped yet. Never give up, no matter how devastating life may seem. Trust God; He will bring you out! Thank You, Lord!!! My number *One, Forever Love*!

Reflection:

What did you learn about others, yourself, the world, or God, from my experience?

CHAPTER 14

BEHIND A VEIL
BY SHANENE HIGGINS

Imagine being in a crowd and wishing you are invisible, but you're marked, and there is nowhere you can hide. I couldn't blend in if my life depended on it. It's said that 4 in 10,000 people worldwide have what the doctors said I had. However, I've never seen one who is disfigured like me, though I know they exist.

I deal with rejection practically every day of my life and have built up an immunity to it over time. However, before building an immunity and not even knowing that there was a problem, I would cover the first bump on the left side of my face.

At first, I thought the lump was an allergic reaction until it didn't go away after some time. I went to a plastic surgeon and had a biopsy. When I returned to the doctor's office, I was informed of the findings. I recall hearing the word Sarcoidosis for the first time. I didn't have a clue as to what it was. When I went back home, I immediately started praying to ask God to heal me. Little did I know that years would go by with no visible sign of healing. More time would pass before another lesion began to appear on my right cheek. At this point, I was extremely stressed out and wondering what in the world was going on as no one in my family had this issue. One year later, another lesion appeared on the right side of my eye. I was so upset, and I became frustrated with the mundane responsibilities of life, like going grocery shopping. Customers would look at me as if I was contagious, and quickly look away as if I was the *ugliest* thing that they had ever seen. There were many times when people would stop and stare at me as if I was a *fish in a fishbowl*. To make matters even worse, children would stare at me while walking toward me with frowns on their faces. Not to mention, elderly men and women would look at me as if I had Ebola! Imagine, if you can, standing out no matter how hard you try to fit in. This is only a fraction of what I've experienced from being physically disfigured.

One afternoon, while walking to one of my favorite natural health food stores (Trader Joe's), I saw a few teenagers walking down the street. When I first saw them, I thought to myself; I should move over to the other side. You see, after being rejected so many times, I just wasn't up to any more rejection, at least not at that moment. But, for some reason, I didn't cross the street. As they came closer to me, the boy that was in the middle of the two girls, yelled out profanities, "Did you see that…on her face!"

My heart ached at the sound of the words leaving his mouth. The two girls kept walking in the other direction. But the boy was walking with his back to them facing me, pointing at both of his cheeks and back at me! Mind you; he was only about 13.

I felt like I had been punched right in the middle of my stomach, and my heart sank as the tears formed in my eyes.

I wondered why this was happening to me. I would later get a glimpse of the reason and purpose of what I was experiencing. But in the meantime, I resorted to trying to hide my face because the lesions were larger than the size of a quarter. I tried to cover them with two First-Aid Circle Band-Aids. Unfortunately, the Band-Aids kept falling off because the lesions were too large. A friend kept telling me that I should stop covering the lesions, but I couldn't bring myself to remove the bandages. As time went on, I stopped trying to hide them even though they were more obvious than in the beginning. Fast forward, *sixteen years* after the first manifestation while I was sitting at The Potter's House, Bishop T. D. Jakes preached a message about Mephibosheth.

"Now Jonathan, Saul's son, had a son crippled in his feet. He was five years old when the report of Saul and Jonathan came from Jezreel, and his nurse took him up and fled. And it happened that in her hurry to flee, he fell and became lame. And his name was Mephibosheth." (2 Samuel 4:4).

I could not believe the timing of that message, because I had recently fallen and broken my leg. At that point, I had to decide if I would remain crippled in the way I saw myself. Would I step out on faith regardless of my face and how others would perceive me, and sing as God had told me to do so many times before?

Would I use the gifts of writing books, songs, music, and screenplays regardless of the horrendous skin lesions, with the possibility of being '*Seen*' and rejected continuously? Would I dare to do what God intentionally purposed me to do?

Time would make all the difference as to what I would do, and how my mind would shift about being stared at daily like a deer stuck in headlights!

Little did I know, I was being prepared for the next level in my life of being stared at on a whole new level by auditing for *The Potter's House Choir* in front of three judges. I was taken aback when one of the judges prophetically spoke into my life about the gifts that God had given me.

I thought to myself, '*He's talking like he's known me for years,*' when he said, "Not only can you sing, you can write, and you're very artistic. You are different than anyone else, and you have your own style. Everything about you is different. Do not change!" He said other things that confirmed I was in alignment with fulfilling my purpose. Mind you; I did not know this man who just happened to be a Grammy Award Winning Producer who *'Saw'* my gifts beyond my flaws. When I exited the room, I was in awe of what God did!

The following Sunday morning, a guest pastor by the name of Keion Henderson preached a powerful message about how being rejected is part of God's plan of protection for those He has called. The message was so powerful; I felt as if God had penned it just for me. Not only has He protected the gifts that He has blessed me with, but He has also protected me. Bishop T.D. Jakes once said that God hides those He has chosen in plain sight. You may think, how is it possible to be hidden in plain sight? Well, God has a tendency of hiding your purpose *Behind a Veil* of rejection until He is ready to release His divine plan for your life.

When I finally began to comprehend somewhat the purpose behind feeling ostracized and rejected, I could rest in knowing that *God's love is too wide and too deep to be without a divine strategy of protection for our lives.* His ultimate intention is to bring His purpose for us to pass for His glory! Rest assured that God will cover you until He delivers you right into the hands of your divine destiny.

His *Divine Strategy* is tailored just for you!

Reflection:

What is it about you that makes you stand out from anyone else that you can now embrace after reading my story?

Chapter 15

Go!
By Tasha Huston

Breathe. Just keep breathing. I felt like I was losing my mind. There. Right there in the middle of my wooden planked hallway, were my planted feet. I stood there on unsteady knees and shaky legs, taking it all in by breathing it all out. Breathe! That word echoed in my earlobes as I went from room to room. The pounding of my heart in my chest threatened to leap out at every voice I heard outside of that door. My friend and I scrambled to take what meant the most to me and stuff it into wide open automobile doors.

I was afraid. I was scared that I would get caught doing something that had to be done for me. The decision was not my doing alone but rather the undoing of the cords to a marriage I could no longer hold together on my own. God stepped in. I didn't want to go, but I felt a tugging to do so. I argued with God at that moment about my life, my purpose, and my audacity to take hold of it to do something unnerving. One word from above kept my trembling feet moving: Go. There are some words from God that will alter the trajectory of your life in such a way that you almost hesitate to move. That movement will require bold faith. There is a sweetness that awaits you when you decide to move forward.

When you stand next to the mountain that *threatens to take you out,* and you say to it, "I don't know why you have come, but I kind of think I'm supposed to be over there and you're in my way, so you know…Move." It's like that.

For me, it was this big overwhelming, knee-shaking movement. Many nights, while sleeping on an unfamiliar couch, looking up at foreign walls, I wondered, *what am I doing?* Instinctively, I wanted to go back to what had become my definition of home. This uncomfortable comfort zone was uneasy. In the weeks that followed, I journeyed deeper within than I had ever gone before, and I selfishly asked, "What do you want?"

As women, often, we neglect this simple question for the sake of others because we have been conditioned to do so. *Don't be selfish. Think of others. Be a lady, always.* After searching the word of God and myself, I realized that what I wanted was vastly different than what I was currently living out. I sat at the kitchen table, telling God I wanted more. His whispered response was audible. I wanted to feel purposeful in every way, and it started with me. Broken me.

It started with me taking a big, bold, brave leap of faith and trusting Him to catch me when I fell flat on my face. It took guts and courage I didn't know I had. That same courage is also within you. When God in all His splendor, says in Jeremiah 1:5, that before He formed you in the womb, He knew you; before you were born, He set you apart; He was not just talking big.

If God, saw fit to set me apart in the beginning, then surely, right here in the middle of this mess I was in, He would show me the way. When I handed Him my marriage and He handed me the outcome, I kept breathing. Deep, slow breaths at first. It was a monumental shift in my life simply because it allowed me to take a good look at the woman I was and the woman I hoped to become.

I developed during that trial in such a way that I am grateful for the painful process of a purposed promise of truly knowing myself.

The most valuable lesson I learned throughout this life-changing event is that I was stronger than I ever gave myself credit to be. *I underestimated the power of me.* Doing that gave others indirect permission to do the same. The strength of God rising within helped me to see the lioness that was there all along. It motivated me to seek environments where my crown could shine and stay away from atmospheres meant to downplay my God-given purpose. I became bolder in my walk with God, my talk with others, and how I lived life. I stopped shrinking myself to make others feel bigger.

I realized that we are all immense and my purpose was too massive to hide any longer. The destiny of my life and the call of God could no longer be denied. I had to honor Him and fulfill my destiny the way He intended.

Before I knew it, my breathing had normalized and within His hand was this beautiful life awaiting me. I stepped bravely into it. In life, there are many decisions you will have to make that will call upon the brave woman within. She will be afraid to take the necessary steps. Take them anyway. *Engage in your freedom and don't let you stop you.* Stand in your truth and know your worth before entering any type of relationship. When you are confident in who you are and what you bring to the table, you are more aware of the value of the seats surrounding you. Not everyone can sit in a Queen's presence. Know that you are the very essence of God's love and that you deserve the best. Be grounded as a woman prior to attaching yourself to a man. He should be the reflection of God that you have in your heart. If he isn't, know that it's okay to walk away. Have the courage to try again and love again.

Don't let a bitter taste in your mouth prevent you from experiencing a better taste of life.

Reflection:

Have you ever been in a relationship that is not in alignment with the call of God on your life, or are you in one now? If so, did you seek direction, if not, are you open to seeking His guidance now?

CHAPTER 16

REDEFINING YOUR PURPOSE
BY LEONA JOHNSON

I am no stranger to adversity. My life was amazing. I had a great job and had been there for ten years! My children are adults. When my youngest went off to college, I was empty-nesting; living it up, enjoying life with a nice car and home with a beautiful yard. My friends and I had gatherings, and I had a peace of mind. Yes, I would say that life was grand. But one day, life as I knew it was interrupted by a phone call while I was working.

"Please come to the office," said my employer.

Imagine my shock when I was told, "Leona, we are laying you off as of Friday."

Boom!!! My entire world had shifted just like that. I had totally unfamiliar thoughts. I was completely lost for words. I was utterly caught off guard. There were so many things going through my head. Although I understood their reasoning, at that moment, nothing prepares you for these sudden life-changing events.

Once reality set in, I had to come up with a game plan. Weeks went by, and I realized job hunting wasn't for me. I had not even tried. I told myself that I was not working for anyone or clocking in at any job. I put myself in a position to start fresh, take all I had and invest in myself to help educate others. I stepped out on faith and launched my company, *Allmannersmatter, LLC.* Being a certified coach and consultant gives me purpose; it is my calling. I love making a difference in others' lives with all the services I provide.

Later that year, I decided to make a few sacrifices in my life, so I could concentrate on my business. I decided to downsize and move away from home. I started packing up, labeling everything and giving some things away. I had to get a storage to hold some things, and other items were going with me in my U-Haul truck.

So now, I am excited about this even newer chapter in my life and *Boom* again! The truck was stolen with everything in it, and the impact of the loss hit me hard! I cannot even describe to you the devastation I was in. Everything I ever worked for; all my personal items, kids' photos, diplomas, yearbooks, my grandmothers' memorandums, my dad's memorandums; gone! What in the world just happened in one year? I had no furniture or anything to move with. I had no choice but to move in with my daughter. Boy oh boy; did I fight this situation? It was very humbling for me, but when you are stuck, you must live with your truth. I felt like I had nothing. I cried silently to myself for a couple of weeks. I knew I had to deal with it, but each time, it got more depressing, and I had phobias about being away from everything I've known for 15 years. I even had hateful and negative thoughts about the men who stole my things. I did not want to talk to anyone. I was in a very dark place. One morning, I woke up to an unfamiliar voice; it was kind of weird, but it was soothing.

The voice said, "Get up, get up! This is not you and what are you going to do about it?"

I thought I was dreaming, but it was so real that I immediately got up. I looked around and felt a sense of energy around me; some type of soothing force. I know it was God!

REDEFINING YOUR PURPOSE

At that moment, I knew I had to tune into my inner thoughts, change my mindset, and get myself together.

I prayed and meditated, "Remove the numbness, remove the anger, remove the anxiety, remove the negative energy." Repeat. Repeat. I confessed this daily until I woke up one day and realized that I felt better and refreshed with the desire to start over. I let go of the things that I lost, realizing that I had more to be grateful for than most. I had a nice home that I lived in, including family and friends that were so supportive during rough times through my journey. Having a supportive family was comforting to me. I started moving through my obstacles one at a time, beginning with the most difficult task. As I began to unleash my life, things became clearer. I remember something my grandmother said to me when I was a teenager,

"Leona, people can say whatever they want to try and hurt you, but they can't take your mind to think and your hands to work…only God can do that."

I never understood that until now. I had to realize that I have every tool I need to get back on my feet. No matter what was taken from me, I was still rich because I had a way to recharge my life. I still believed that all things were possible and that I was destined for greatness. I was free to move forward and be the winner of my life. I began working on the things I needed to do, including restarting my company and redirecting my personal affairs.

I am supercharged now and not looking back. When you lose material things that you value that you can never get back, you gain a new perspective of what is valuable. I value grace and favor in my life now. I'm grateful for all I have daily. I'm living through my testimony of overcoming obstacles that seemed insurmountable.

Keep your Heavenly Father first in all things, and your purpose will be attracted to you. Believe in yourself. Believe in your truth.

Grace and favor worked for me as I did these three things:

- I made a choice.
- I took a chance.
- I made a change

…and *you* can too!

Reflection:

Do you believe grace and favor can pull you through, if so why?

CHAPTER 17

NOTHING IS WASTED
BY NORA MACIAS

It has been said that "Children are like wet cement." Nothing could be closer to my reality. I was born and raised in church–a small, legalistic church where, basically, being left-handed was a sin. Although I claimed to have been 'saved' at the early age of 8, I never really *knew* God. I never knew who I truly was *in Him*.

Born of first-generation Mexican immigrants, I was one of five siblings. Four were born fair-skinned, and I was born with olive skin. I did not know that, in those days, to be dark-skinned was not a good thing. Or so my mother thought. Hence, she nicknamed me 'La Morena' (The Dark-Skinned One) and said, "*Que fea!*" ("How *ugly!*"), when she saw me at birth. This became my truth. It took root deep in my heart, and soon, the ugly weeds began to manifest.

I learned very early on that I had to 'perform' to gain acceptance and approval. After trying on light face powders, yo-yo dieting, and reading self-improvement books, I thought: "*Since I can't be beautiful, I'll just be smart!*" And I did just that—I became very studious. I graduated from a local university with honors and began a career in Sales. I entered every contest and pageant imaginable, both in my career and church, and won most of them. While the awards, trophies and crowns were piling up, I could *not* get my mom to ever say, "I'm proud of you!" I began the never-ending road to becoming the ever-so-tired perfectionist.

Soon, I began to blossom. I had no idea I was quite beautiful. Regardless, that was not what *I* saw in the mirror. I saw 'the rejected one.' I became 'the desperate one,' and so, I began *Looking for Love in all the Wrong Places*. I slowly became resentful and rebellious. As a result, drama became a way of life for me. If it didn't exist, I created it, and sabotage became a pattern.

Three molestations later—by a family friend, a stranger in the park, and a doctor, I started a collection of secrets, never to be told. Isolation and more unhealthy patterns led to abortions and later date rape. The night I was raped was Christmas Eve.

I don't remember which was more terrifying—waking up, not knowing where I was, or the look on my 5-year-old's face the next morning, when he saw there were no presents under the tree.

After experiencing infidelity and divorce, I was now raising a son on my own. My son was the silver lining; he was the gift that I could not believe I deserved. So, as most single moms do, I worked day and night, struggling to make ends meet.

My amazing son was now a teen, and after abandonment by my second (alcoholic) husband, I felt like such a failure. I had nothing left but brokenness. It was as if a dark cloud was hovering over me and all the while, I was crying out: "Why me?"

My past haunted me with guilt and shame. Unbeknownst to me, those events had opened the door to the 'transferring of spirits,' and demonic manifestations began to unfold!

I, mistakenly, believed the fallacy that Christians could not be demonized, nor need deliverance. Therefore, I never talked about it. I just continued my Christian walk with the Lord, not knowing torment awaited me for years to come.

Having grown tired of legalism, one day, I heard my brother-in-law talking about a 'Mega-Church' in San Jose, California called Jubilee Christian Center, and things began to turn. There, I was given a prophetic word that "My Boaz was coming in 2015." This had always been my heart's desire! Of course, the enemy tried to derail me, and I fell for a *'counterfeit'* man who further disappointed me. I became very discouraged. I was done! In fact, I was quite mad at God! My two best friends became *anger and rage*. I was tired of hearing phrases like: "*Nothing is wasted!*" and "God is always on time!" Well...on December 30, 2015, God *was* on time! My *Boaz* arrived, and everything changed.

He exemplified how to 'love me like Christ.' He accepted me, broken and all, with unconditional love. He didn't try to *fix* me; he just *loved* me. Little did I know that *I* was a dream come true *for him*. Who, me? The crazy woman? —The basket case? Yes, *me*!

Shortly into our marriage, he introduced me to his spiritual mother, Lois, and it was then I began my journey towards deliverance. I participated in an inner-healing program, where three anointed women led me to *the truth*—the truth about *who I am* in Christ. I received breakthrough, after breakthrough, and I began to heal. I learned to *identify* the lies that came in, *how* they entered, and *what* to do about them. The result was true freedom!

Now I *know* who I am. I have a new heart. I walk victoriously in the creative gifts God has given me, and I have a burning desire to share. I now minister to women with wounded hearts. By helping women discover *who they are in Christ*, I have witnessed inner-healing in the physical, emotional and spiritual realms, including demonic deliverance!

I am living proof of Romans 8:28—*All* things work together for good—and it's true...*nothing is wasted!*

I am *His divine design*, and now I get to bless other *Women of Purpose* with my creative gifts. As I like to say, "I used to be a basket case…now I make them!"

God has changed my name to Norah—that's Nora with an 'h.' It means 'light of God,' for I *am* no longer in the dark!

The once labeled 'Ugly One' has found her 'Beauty for Ashes.' The 'Crazy Woman,' turned 'Amazing Woman,' is now walking in her Purpose!

Reflection:

What are the *lies* that are keeping *you* from *your* purpose?

CHAPTER 18

GIRL, ME TOO!
BY LEANDRA MCLAURIN

As a child, I was always encouraged to dream big, treat others how I wanted to be treated and that I could do anything I put my mind to. So me being me, I dreamed big! By the time I was in high school, I had a plan: graduate college at 20 (I did by the grace of God), be established in my dream career by 22, meet the love of my life at 23, get married by 25, dream house by 26, have my first child by 27, child number 2 by 30, and live happily ever after. HA!

You know how the saying goes, you make plans, and God laughs. God must have been cracking up when I made these plans. I mean that gut-busting, can't breathe, tears rolling down your face type of laugh! So, here I am at 28, debt up to my ears, not married, no children, barely getting this adulthood thing to go in my favor, and *finally* have a stable job I love.

I always ask myself, why didn't anyone tell me life was this hard?! Why is being an adult so, ugh! I miss the days where I could ask for what I want, and nine times out of ten, I would get it! Born to a single mother, I was an only child surrounded by the love of my mother, grandmother, aunts, and cousins. When I tell you we're close, we're close! I have two cousins that are basically my siblings. Holidays were *always* spent together, and the occasional family vacation. I'm a mama's girl through and through, and my granny was the glue that held us all together.

My father was in and out of my life; I saw him most holidays and birthdays, but around the age of 10 is when things took a turn. My father passed away in 2001. It was very sudden for me; one day he was fine, I was going to his car shop and playing with the dogs there. Then the next thing I know, he's in the hospital very ill, drinking some type of green juice and calling me his "golden child." What's going on here? The next time mom and I went to visit him in the hospital, he expired. I will never forget those words from the nurse because I didn't know what the term expired meant.

He's gone, just like that. No manual, no guidance, no information on who he was, what he liked, and how to live in a world without him. Nothing! *Don't get me wrong, we weren't close, but that doesn't mean that I didn't want my daddy.* What little girl doesn't want the love and attention of her father? Who was going to be my example of a man? I didn't know this at the time of his passing, but as I got older, I realized I really need my daddy. I struggled with my weight even as a young child, sought the attention and approval from others, and lacked communication skills because of my need to please everyone. I let others define my beauty; I would try to impress others, not for myself but to get the attention that I deeply yearned for from my dad. I wanted that relationship with him, that bond, and connection that I have with my mom. To this day, I still at times want my daddy.

Fast forward to 2010. I graduated from college, turned 21, and the death of my beloved granny. Her death was the straw that broke the camel's back. I fell into a depression. Not only did I lose a piece of my heart but to top it all off, I didn't have a job after college. Isn't that the point of going to college to get a well-paying job when you graduate?! I was bamboozled and sold a dream, but I digress.

Back to my granny, she held it all together. I felt that after we lost her, my family would fall apart, and in a way, we did. Holidays were never the same. The first year after her death, we kept the tradition of being together, but there was no reason for us to come together like that anymore; everyone had their own lives and families. Holidays, especially Christmas dinner, would now consist of mom and me. My heart broke, and my abandonment issue started to rear its ugly head. My fear of being left alone in this world became very present.

So, you can only imagine the pressure I placed on myself. I set high expectations for myself, trying to be perfect in all I do, and when I didn't meet my standards, that's when I became my own worst enemy. My weight crept up, and my self-esteem went down. I felt alone, not physically alone, but emotionally and spiritually.

I felt like God abandoned me and that He wasn't listening to me. Every time I think that things are changing in the right direction, 'Bam,' I take ten steps back. It wasn't until about three years ago when I realized that I couldn't control everything; life is what it is. I had to let go and trust in God. That's when I left a job that was literally killing me; I had stress and anxiety 'Every Day!' I spent an average of 3 hours in L.A. traffic daily going to and from work. I was exhausted, and I had to save my own life, so I quit! It was one of the hardest decisions I had ever made because I didn't have a backup plan, and I always have a plan! No job waiting for me, 'Nothing!' That's when my life changed.

God wanted me to trust Him, so here I am trusting God. I posted my resume on almost every job board there is, went on interviews and nothing. I applied for a city job a few months before I officially quit. Not really feeling qualified, I applied anyway and took a chance. When I tell you God is good, He's good 'All' the time. I got an email for an interview about a week after I quit my job. This job was mine! Fast forward a couple of months, I get the job I knew was for me, and I can say I am truly happy with what I do and who I serve. I work for a program that I believe in and love the people who I work with and for. As a Health Educator, I started to think of ways to take what I'm learning at work and incorporate it into my own life. I began looking into coaching, specifically life coaching, and just like that, I decided to create something for millennial women like myself who have struggled with their body image and low self-esteem.

This year, I have started my own coaching business to help other women learn to love the skin they're in by healing their relationship with their bodies and showing up powerfully in all areas of their lives. I want to show you that you don't have to struggle alone and that you can jumpstart a life that you have always dreamed of!

Through all the ups and downs, highs and lows, I can say I am different; a complete turnaround from what I came from. I am comfortable in my own skin, learning something new about myself every day, loving my body and who I am becoming. If you get anything from my story, it's not allowing your past to define you. Don't quit! Even when things are going all wrong, do not give up the fight and have faith. My story could have turned out differently; I could have been someone I don't recognize today, but by the grace of God and because of the love and support I am surrounded by, I am here. I am working to better myself and those around me.

My purpose is to shed light on this dark world, bring joy and a sense of community to women through the experiences of 'Girl, Me Too! My story isn't finished, it's just the beginning.

Reflection:

How is your story just beginning?

CHAPTER 19

NO MATTER THE CIRCUMSTANCES
BY SHIRLYON MCWHORTER

I was like a child on Christmas day sitting in my plush office on the penthouse floor in the city of Coral Gables, known as The City Beautiful where the streets are lined with beautiful trees, monumental buildings, green space, winding roadways, and houses that you only see in magazines. I spent the first two hours talking to anyone who walked into the breakroom. It was not until the senior law partner asked me if I intended to do any work that I decided to go to my office. For some unknown reason, I was unable to concentrate on work. I had this feeling that something special was about to happen.

At about 11:57 am, I heard the secretary, who was covering the front desk yelling my name. She was obviously having problems operating the telephone.

"Shirlyon, you have a call on line two, she shouted."

The voice on the phone was one that I recognized, the 43rd Governor of Florida, Jeb Bush.

He said hello Ms. McWhorter. I replied, Hi Governor Bush, how are you today. I knew it was going to happen. I had been waiting for this call for years. In his gubernatorial voice, he asked, how would you like to be a County Court Judge? I screamed as loud as I could. This was a shock because I always said that I would remain cool, calm and collective when I received the call. Would that be a yes? Yes, yes Mr. Governor. I later learned that he told President Bronson of Bethune-Cookman University that he appointed an alum as a judge and she has a good set of lungs.

That my friend is how the story began. It was one of the most exciting days of my life. I had finally reached the top of my game. Yes, I had arrived! My humble beginnings lead me from the country town of Wauchula, Florida where I picked oranges after school to the courtroom where I served as a role model for the litigants that appeared before me. Service to others matter.

I learned early in life that there are no dreams too big to dream! We have been given everything we need to create the life we desire and deserve. We must focus, see ourselves beyond our circumstances, make good decisions, minimize distractions, create a dream team and express gratitude daily. I have never denied my meager beginnings. However, I learned that my circumstances do not define me. You see, at a very young age, I made a conscious effort to live outside of my circumstances. I am a dreamer.

The fact that I did not know any Black lawyers, judges or police did not hinder me. I began my legal career as an Assistant State Attorney with the Dade County State Attorney's office in "County Court," where I later served as a Judge. I was chosen as one of the first prosecutors to serve as an attorney for the newly formed full-time Domestic Violence Court in the State of Florida. I later joined the legal staff of the Dade County Police Benevolent Association where I was quickly promoted to Assistant General Counsel. I represented over 6,000 corrections and law enforcement officers. I did it because I believed I could. My parents each had a high school diploma. That did not stop me from graduating Summa

NO MATTER THE CIRCUMSTANCES

Cum Laude at Bethune-Cookman College and Thank You Lawdy from the University of Florida College of Law.

The path to living your dream is never a straight line. There will always be detours, turns and roadblocks. And I certainly had my share along the way! But nothing would prepare me for the stop sign that was thrown in front of me four years later during the excitement of the election. When I saw the vote count flash across the television, I felt like I had been hit by an eighteen-wheeler. I lost the election. The family that had comforted me my entire life no longer made a difference. My mom, brothers, sisters, and friends were all there to witness this public humiliation.

I felt like I had been shot with an AK47. A dull ache surrounded my heart for the following three days. While others left to return home, my dear mother remained behind to take care of her child. Each day she would come to my bedroom to offer me food. She tried to get me to talk to the many friends that reached out via telephone. Nothing worked. I did not open my door for three days and three nights.

What just happened? How could God who had given me my dream job allow it to be taken away by someone who added a Hispanic name to run and barely qualified? Where was the justice in this? I have yet to find it, but I got up from my bed on the third day more determined than ever to live my best life. My mom and I went shopping and had lunch at a new restaurant that I wanted to try. After all, this was a time of new beginnings. This was the worse day of my life, but this is not how the story ends.

During my time of reflection, I realized I got up on the third day which is significant to me as a believer. According to, Hosea 6:2, he will revive and restore us on the third day. Some things that I know for sure is that I have learned lessons from defeat. I am stronger in my faith because of what I went through. It was a character building experience. I also learned for sure that you can and you will recover from loss and losing. My time on the bench continues to open doors to people and places as I inspire others to live the life they desire and deserve.

Reflection:

What circumstances have you allowed to control your life? How can you re-direct your reactions to your situation today to determine your destiny tomorrow?

CHAPTER 20

A HEART THAT FORGIVES
BY MICHELE MILLS

God's heartbeat is gracious. It is merciful, slow to anger, and of great kindness. Jonah was familiar with these attributes of God. However, he became angry with God simply because he did not get his way with the people of Nineveh. God still showed compassion for Jonah despite his ways (Jonah 4:1-11; NIV).

This goes to show us that regardless of how we may feel about a certain city, culture, or individual, God has the last word. He has a heart full of great compassion and love for His people.

Jonah did not have the heartbeat of God. He did not have the compassion of God for the people. He knew of God, but he lacked intimacy. How many people know of God, know of His Word, and know of His people, but do not know Him? They lack intimacy.

How do we become intimate with the Holy Spirit? I am glad that you asked. We become intimate with the Holy Spirit by spending time with God and reading His Word. Intimacy requires us to have a relationship with our Heavenly Father, consisting of communicating with Him, crying out in prayer, acknowledging Him in all our ways, and continually seeking His face. In other words, by "letting our hair down" in worship.

Becoming intimate with the Holy Spirit is a process. The more we draw close to God, the more God draws close to us. His Spirit will go deeper and deeper within us, and His seed will start to grow. We will become "spiritually pregnant" with God's seed—His Spirit.

The Bible says that "Adam *knew* his wife Eve, and she conceived." (Genesis 4:1 and 25). This should encourage you to guard, protect, and nourish what the Lord has placed within you. Ultimately, this growing intimacy will cause God's love to spring forth like rivers of living water. You will begin to have a deep love for the things of God...His heartbeat. Having His heartbeat will birth the desire within to fulfill your purpose in life.

Intimacy with the Lord will cause His power to freely flow within your heart. He gives the power to forgive, to dismiss 'all' false accusations, to be merciful, to be gracious, to be slow to anger, and to extend loving kindness to all people.

For example, Gina and I attend a local church, and we had a disagreement. We had not taken the time to mend our differences with each other. Gina, who is a member of the church's leadership team and a singer in the choir, started sharing her side of the story with others. I sat back and kept silent. However, I noticed that everyone associated with Gina's sphere of influence started treating me with animosity or bitterness. Some of the other church members who had heard some of the gossips, started to treat me differently also. A certain group of church members begins to slander my name. Undesirably, they would separate me from all social gatherings. Crazy enough, at the church fellowships, they intentionally did not sit at the same table with me, or even sit beside me during the church service. It was as though I was a castaway. The people treated me the same way that they treated Jonah. They justified their actions and truly believed that their ways were right, just as the Pharisees (the "religious" folks) did with our Lord Jesus Christ when they crucified Him on the cross.

"Blessed are ye, when men shall hate you, and when they shall separate you from their company, and shall reproach you, and cast your name out as evil, for the Son of man's sake." (Luke 6:22; KJV).

Despite this treatment, I kept praying, serving God, and attending church. I cried out to God daily saying, "Why Lord? Why are they treating me in this manner?"

I thought, how can people think it is right to pick and choose who they should love and accept? What kind of love is this?

Some people feel as though they can treat other people any kind of way. They backbite, are envious of one another, and yet they still have the notion to speak in tongues, display their prophetic gifts, fathom all mysteries and all knowledge, show faith that can move mountains but do not have love for one another.

I am a firm believer that there are two sides to every story, and then there are the facts. Just because someone tells you one thing doesn't make it always the true version. If you are not willing or able to listen to both sides of a story, do not be so quick to make judgment on what you have not heard.

God's heartbeat showers us with love known as His 'Agape' love. It is a self-giving and sacrificial love that seeks the good of another. A love that is careful of other people's feelings and reputation. It denies oneself to promote one another. What greater love is it for a man or woman to lay down their lives for one another? This love is the heartbeat of God, and it needs to be practiced in all nationalities and most importantly, the churches. For God is *Love*.

"For this is the original message we heard: We should love each other. We must not be like Cain, who joined the Evil One and then killed his brother. And why did he kill him? Because he was deep in the practice of evil,

while the acts of his brother were righteous. So, don't be surprised, friends, when the world hates you. This has been going on a long time." (1 John 3:11-13; MSG).

Nineteen years ago, I vowed to God to walk in forgiveness, and not bitterness. Regardless of the number of times I am hurt or offended by a person's words or actions, I am determined to forgive. Having a *Heart that Forgives* is so essential to my God-ordained purpose in my ministry. I praise God that over time, walking in forgiveness has become a lifestyle. Living a lifestyle of forgiveness, most certainly, keeps the heart free to flow without bitterness and negativity. Forgiveness helps us love without holding a grudge. It helps us release a person, instead of holding them in handcuffs to their mistake.

Forgiving individuals who have mistreated us is one of the most challenging things God expects us to achieve. Forgiving the trivial offenses and insults can be stress-free, however, what if the attack against you is so excruciating it appears unforgivable? How can you forgive a person who hurt someone you love or broke your precious heart? On the other hand, unforgiveness spreads like wildfire. This unforgiving virus will infect everyone you encounter. Sadly, you will become a prisoner to the situation at hand and not be able to fulfill your purpose. An unforgiving heart continues to spread like the plague. This is a true statement, "Hurt people hurt people, and misery loves company."

Choose today which principle you will allow to occupy your mind. Stop, and look at the woman in the mirror.

Reflection:
Be honest with yourself.

- How has forgiveness or unforgiveness affected your relationships?
- Close your eyes and think of someone you need to forgive?
- How many relationships have you destroyed, for you or others, because of your unforgiveness?
- Have you ever done anything that you need God to forgive you for?
- Do you want to let it go?
- What are you going to do differently to get free from the pain of the past?
- Decide today to live a lifestyle of forgiveness and not bitterness.

"For if you forgive [a]others their trespasses [their reckless and willful sins], your heavenly Father will also forgive you. 15 But if you do not forgive others [nurturing your hurt and anger with the result that it interferes with your relationship with God], then your Father will not forgive your trespasses" (Matthew 6:14-15: AMP).

"At that point, Peter got up the nerve to ask, "Master, how many times do I forgive a brother or sister who hurts me? Seven?" Jesus replied, "Seven! Hardly. Try seventy times seven" (Matthew 18:21-22; MSG).

CHAPTER 21

THE JOURNEY TO PURPOSE
BY DR. NGOZI M. OBI

"*Purpose,*" is generally defined as the reason we were created or why we are on this earth. Everyone craves purpose, and seriously, who does not want to know the very reason they were born? We all do, and the Word gives us a glimpse into our destiny.

"*For I know the plans I have for you, declares the LORD, plans to prosper you and not to harm you, plans to give you hope and a future.*" (Jeremiah 29:11; NIV).

With a promise like that, why is it that we do not delve right into our *purpose-driven life*? I dare to say that fear holds most of us back. Whether it be fear of rejection, fear of failing in life or some other type of dread; the bottom line is fear. Fear can be crippling, and when experienced with devastating results, it causes many to give up and not try again because they are terrified that what happened the first time will happen again.

Think about the fear of rejection. We all naturally crave acceptance because it usually means we have achieved our goals and have arrived at our desired destination in life. If during the process of mapping out our destiny, we happen to get rejected, then for some; it means they are not on the right path. How wrongfully so a thought that is. Truth be told, many people will not see your potential in life until it is fully developed. Just because others do not see your potential does not mean you have missed your life's path. It is up to you to prove naysayers wrong when presenting ideas to others backfire and they cannot see where your life is headed. So, if at first you fail in your quest or experience rejection, do not give up and say, "Woe is me." Simply ask God where you went wrong and how to correct it. Also ask for those who will see your vision and help you achieve it. Be bold and try again.

When I started my journey as an author, I shared with someone at a prayer meeting that I felt I should write fiction. She immediately shot my idea down and told me that self-help books are what I should be writing. My spirit was disturbed by her words. I left the prayer meeting and went to God in prayer. After a few days, God showed me how every time Jesus preached a sermon in the New Testament; His points were hidden in parables. What is a parable but a short story? That revelation armed me to pursue my purpose in writing regardless of what anybody else says. Anytime someone rejects my vision and tries to shut me down; I have a reference that reminds me of what I am supposed to be doing and encourages me to stay the course.

"Whether you turn to the right or to the left, your ears will hear a voice behind you, saying, "This is the way; walk in it." (Isaiah 30:21; NIV).

"I will instruct you and teach you in the way you should go; I will counsel you with my loving eye on you." (Psalms 32:8; NIV).

God promises to guide us in the way we are supposed to walk in life. We only need to believe and trust what He says to us and walk in it regardless of whether other people see our vision or not. Even if we do not know how we are going to succeed in our purpose, we can trust He who ordained our path in life before we were formed in our mother's womb. *He is faithful to cause us to fulfill our purpose and bring us to our desired end.* We need not fear rejection or failure.

Notably, God also told me not to despise small beginnings when I started writing. I admit that I did not completely understand what He was saying back then. However, four published books later, I now fully understand what He meant. He simply meant that there is no longevity in short-term success.

If one genuinely wants to make a mark on this world through their purpose and leave a legacy by building something that will last for generations to come, one must persevere through small beginnings.

Another thing that holds us back from fulfilling destiny is complacency or comfortability with where we already are in life. Do not get me wrong; I am all about savoring the ride of life.

After all, it is intended to be a journey instead of merely reaching a destination. Remembering to savor the journey is important because, at times, we get antsy, wanting to reach our destination in such a hurry that we fail to enjoy the ride and ultimately miss the right path to our purpose. We forget that the ride there is part of fulfilling our life's purpose and just as significant as getting to our desired destination.

We should definitely *stop and smell the roses* along the road to purpose, but we should never 'park' there. This brings me back to my earlier point about complacency and comfortability. Some are not willing to do the work required to achieve purpose while others get a taste of success and 'park' there. They do not continue to the next level because they become comfortable with what they have achieved thus far. They fail to realize that there is still more to be attained. Anyone serious about fulfilling purpose should be mindful of these traps.

Motion is constant and necessary when pursuing purpose because destiny is achieved in levels. That is why we never get our next assignment until the previous one is complete.

Reflection:

Have you been complacent about beginning your purpose-filled journey or are you parked on your road to destiny because you are too comfortable or afraid?

Never let the mirage of fear or the taste of initial success cloud your vision. The world awaits!

CHAPTER 22

CHASING A DREAM
BY BEVERLY REYNOLDS

I recall in high school that learning to play music did not come easily to me, a clarinetist in the concert band. Although I had a passion for the arts, practicing rarely seemed to fit into my social schedule. Time with friends at sporting events was a higher priority. One time, I even laid my clarinet on the grandstand beside me. The crowd went wild, and the vibrations sent my instrument crashing to the floor. It wasn't until I had to pay a huge financial price did I even start to care for my investment.

Fast forward to my sophomore year; our high school director announced that the symphonic band would soon be traveling to Florida for a week-long tour playing prestigious tunes and going to Disney World.

The highlight of the trip would be performing in the outdoor pavilion of the World Showcase at Epcot. My eyes imagined every second of what it would be like from the audience to meeting Mickey Mouse. At the time, I had only visited Disney World once with my family and longed to return, not just as a visitor, but as a performer. However, there were a few challenges that stood in my way of this dream.

First, I was in the concert band and needed to prove that I was worthy of a seat in the symphonic band. Second, there were six people ahead of me that I had to set an individual playoff appointment to pass each in the lineup. Both had to be completed with time to raise money and purchase a formal gown.

This meant setting an appointment with the person in the next seat and the director, and then repeating that five times. It also required practicing and playing the new music better than my opponent. The end goal was to make it to at least the last seat in the formally-structured band.

The symphonic band had a reputation for processing on and off stage in neat, orderly conduct. Every female had a formal black gown with formal jewelry. The males had black tuxedos with satin-lined pants and white shirts with cufflinks. Each member 'looked the part.'

Every night, I would come home from school and complete my homework as fast as I could. Then, to my parents' amazement, I was not only finding time to practice but was playing harder music. Admittedly, they had to have a lot of patience while I squeaked out bad notes and horrible renditions of the same runs. I told my parents about my plan to perform at Disney World. My parents were not only patient, but they encouraged me daily to meet my goal. I knew they would never let me quit my dream. Soon enough, the first payoff date arrived. My opponent, director and I sat in a room with all the music for the next seat up. My opponent was defending their seat, while I sought to pass them in the lineup. The director would choose any bar and ask us to play the same notes and decide who played the best at the end.

My first session did not come easily, but in the end, I surpassed my opponent. I was one step closer to making my dream a reality. Over the coming weeks, I would have four more playoffs just to get to the top of the concert band. One-by-one, I had more challenging opponents until I reached the top of my section of the concert band. The final challenge was to secure a playoff with the last seat in the third chair of the symphonic band. Practicing meant taking on a whole new level of music and playing it better than my newest opponent. I knew that once I made it in the band, I would never have to fight to stay in the band. Instead, I would have a new challenge of meeting the higher standards.

I requested the sheet music and took it home with pride. That very evening, I opened the folder and immediately became overwhelmed by the premier piece, *The 1812 Overture*. This piece was long with tough clarinet runs. I was silent for the first time during my nightly practice. I recall my mother coming into my room and asking to see the music. Without letting a second pass, she said, "This is not much different than your old music, just take one note of each run at a time. Be deliberate about learning each note, then put it together."

My mother always had a way of simplifying problems into attainable chunks. I only had a two-week timeframe to learn the music and convince the director I belonged in the symphonic band. I could *not* read music, so I solicited the help of my father, an avid accordion player proficient at reading music as if the notes danced on the page. He would play a few bars and then ask me to repeat.

My mother and my father both inspired me never to give up! My dad would tell me that school was the easiest job I would ever have in life. Looking back, I am not sure how my parents had the patience while I continuously played wrong notes and cried.

Each time I cried, my parents would push me to keep going. After the first week leading to the final challenge, I realized how far I had come. There was only one week until my final challenge. It was the only chance I had to make it to the symphonic band. Soon enough, the day had come for me to put my practice to the test. I gave everything I had to each measure and note. At the end of the session, the director looked at me and said, "Welcome to the band! You will be playing with us in a few weeks at Disney World."

I was overcome with joy and knew that my *relentlessness* paid off. A few weeks later, we processed onto the World Showcase stage. My director raised his wand, the music commenced, and the gong rang resoundingly backstage.

I had *Chased my Dream* and caught it and so can you. Never give up!

Reflection:

Have you ever stopped short of chasing your dreams and how does this story encourage you never to give up?

CHAPTER 23

THE MEETING PLACE
BY TIFFANY RICHARDS

I will never forget the day that my purpose found me! It was not by way of a glamorous or elaborate scene nor was it an epiphany that arose from a moment of inspiration. My purpose arrived at my door unannounced, knocking when I wasn't ready to answer. It came at a time of my deepest despair. You see, everyone wants to discover their life's meaning or at least have an idea. However, no one explains that sometimes, the journey will take you places your heart isn't prepared for. Most often, purpose exists on the other side of healing. This was my experience.

When it came to my future, I had a master plan. I fell victim to the spirit of comparison and was held captive by the timeline I predetermined to keep up with those around me. I would get married, have kids, establish my dream career, score the house, car, and whatever else signified a successful life all by the age of 30. As I began to follow this blueprint, I failed to realize that I never even considered God's will for my life. I silenced the gentle whisper trying to get my attention and instead pushed through my poor decisions all in efforts to reach my misguided goal.

All the red flags that I collected along the way would come back to haunt me once reality set in.

It wasn't long, five years after marriage to be exact, that my world came crashing down around me. I was a divorced mom of a 3-year-old that had to start over and learn how to adapt to her new normal. I was lost, confused, and distressed.

I began to ask myself, "How did I get here?"

God asked me if I was ready, ready to listen, ready to follow. The last few years were spent as a student as I studied my life in hindsight. It was like my mind entered a time machine of thought travel, taking me back to the day I decided that my plan was better than God's. I'll be honest, the truth at times was hard to swallow, but it became the nourishment my soul needed to heal. I realized all the times I ignored my intuition and better judgment getting in my way, rushing the pace of my destiny when I had no idea where I was headed. From dating until and throughout marriage, I drifted. I wasn't praying, worshipping, attending church, or taking time to be in His presence. I agreed to things that I knew were against my morals and upbringing. I justified my sin to give myself a false peace of mind. I had become so deeply rooted in my flesh that I couldn't even feel or hear God anymore.

Even still, He was always there, patiently waiting for me to invite Him into my mess. He knew all along where I would end up, and never let go of me even when I let go of Him. Owning my truth was the first step in moving forward. While I could have allowed my circumstances to keep me bound to brokenness, I decided to do the work. It took a season of solitude for me to become reacquainted with my Savior while He loved me whole again.

I embraced my singleness and saw it as a gift instead of a burden. I began to trust His timing and His plan. Divine connections were made with people who poured into me and aided in my transformation.

I entered therapy to address the wounds from my divorce that led to the uncovering of unresolved childhood traumas. Gradually and gracefully, I was finally becoming the woman that I was created to be. This happened only after I came to *the end of myself* and surrendered to the calling on my life. I celebrated my progress, appreciated my process, and acknowledged my pain because it all led me here. As a result, I gained more clarity on my assignment.

My passion for writing that I had abandoned for over a decade was reignited. My social media platforms became a forum for connecting to the hearts of others with my words. I started a blog to help those on their path to healing. Friends and strangers alike began to reach out to me, asking for guidance with relationship dilemmas. It all started to make sense, that everything I had endured was not in vain and was beyond me. I was to use my testimony to encourage seasons of healthy singleness, godly dating, and anointed marriages. My experiences and lessons learned would save someone else from making the same mistakes.

I was able to tell other hurting souls how to achieve wholeness by referencing my own restoration. More importantly, my primary message would be to wait on God and seek Him above all else. It was amazing to me to see how what I had been through was working for good. To think that all I wanted was to one day feel better and come out of my situation in one piece. All along, I was being positioned to receive the promises of my future.

I have learned that it was never about me inviting Him in because He was always there. No matter how far away I felt at times, He created a *meeting place* right where I was. He was never surprised by my stumbles or falls, and He was always willing to carry me until I could stand securely on my own. The valleys, the detours, were all the same—an opportunity for Him to become reacquainted with me again. It was the atmosphere I needed that awakened me to my purpose.

Reflection:

How has waiting or not waiting on God affected your life? What steps are you taking to trust God more and allow Him full access? Are there areas in your life that are harder to surrender than others?

CHAPTER 24

SHE CHOSE PURPOSE
BY JASMINE SPRATT-CLARKE

She was 21 years old with her whole life ahead of her. Yet, she was broken, abused and misguided. She was pregnant by a man that she thought loved her. After years of saying he wanted a family, her child's father decided he no longer wanted their baby. She was afraid because as a preacher's daughter, this was not the kind of news you return home from college to tell your parents.

As a single parent, it was a daily challenge for her balancing college courses and a newborn. Things became so hard for her financially. One day, she called her child's father and asked if he could buy pampers because she didn't have any money. He fussed and finally told her that he wasn't going to buy pampers. She couldn't understand why he had become so hateful and mean. It became apparent that he enjoyed the idea of feeling needed by her. Angry from the call with her child's father, she walked into a Dollar General Store in Oxford, Mississippi, and contemplated stealing pampers for her 6-month-old son. Although she didn't have a dime to her name, she knew stealing was not the answer. What she didn't realize was that God would later send two angels to help her care for her son. Her mother and Aunt Caroline stepped in and took care of her son so that she could attend classes and work part-time.

One lesson that she learned early was to be grateful for the people who God sends to help you. She worked and attended classes as a full-time student, never taking a semester off. She graduated with a degree in journalism. Soon after, she began applying for internships and entry-level positions. She landed an interview for a public relations role in Mobile, Alabama. She accepted the interview and a week later, received an offer for a full-time paid internship.

After accepting the offer, she was ready to pack her bags and move to Mobile. She found a nice apartment close to work and looked forward to her first day at her new job. The day came, and she drove to the new job, only to find that no one was there. The office was empty. The back and forth emails with her boss continued for four weeks as she tried to understand why she hadn't started working. She couldn't understand why her manager would hire her for a role and then disappear.

She moved four hours away from home only to end up sleeping on the floor of her new apartment in a city where she didn't know anyone. After the first few weeks with no income from the internship, she pulled herself up and began looking for another job. But all she found was a part-time retail position at BCBG. She went to work every day depressed because it wasn't what she wanted, and she hated being without her son. She couldn't afford childcare on a part-time salary, so her son had to continue living with her parents during this time. 2012 was one of the hardest years of her life. During this valley experience, she read her Bible and prayed fervently. No bed, little to no income, and a child to raise.

Four months later, she landed a full-time community relations role at a non-profit in Mobile earning about $33,000 per year. She began to travel for work, meet new people and see life in a different light. She was finally able to move her son to Mobile. During this time, she met an amazing man who later became the father figure

SHE CHOSE PURPOSE

that she desired for her son. But even with the full-time income, finances were still tight, so she decided to leave Mobile to pursue a corporate career in Atlanta.

Her valley season had taught her to trust God fully. She moved to Atlanta with no job, merely faith. She was able to live with her sister until she found a job. She landed a marketing role at a Fortune 500 company in Atlanta. As time went on, she began landing more corporate roles that continued to elevate her. In three years, her salary doubled from when she was working at the non-profit in Mobile. She was working hard, thriving and her life was poppin'...until the summer of 2016.

She lost her corporate job and was unemployed for four months with rent three times the amount she paid while living in Mobile. Although she received unemployment, it was not enough income to take care of her bills and her son. She figured this would be another time she and her son would have to visit the Salvation Army for groceries. In 2016, her gross income was less than her non-profit salary, but with double the bills living in Atlanta. She received government assistance for food and healthcare. This season of her life felt all too familiar. But this time, she didn't feel strong enough to get through it. But God is faithful.

One day, her good friend, Zakiyrah, asked if she knew someone who could edit her new book. She thought about it and figured she could do it since editing is what she'd done for years in her career. What she didn't know was that this editing opportunity would lead her to birth a new business, theJSbrand.

At the intersection of her unemployment, her passion for writing and helping others was her *purpose*. Her gifts collided with her destiny. She survived single parenting, public shame, seasons of unemployment, a toxic relationship with her child's father and so much more. But she isn't a victim. She's a *victor*. The Word is true, what you reap in tears, you sow in joy.

Today, she is a wife to the amazing man she met in Mobile, a writer, and a successful businesswoman, all because she decided to trust God and go for it. She is me! *Purpose is waiting on the other side of your fear.*

Reflection:

What purpose is standing on the other side of what appears to be impossible for you to accomplish?

CHAPTER 25

HER FREEDOM
BY SHAUNIC STANFORD

The boulders I carried for years vanished with one hit of the gavel. A wave of relief overwhelmed me as I exited the courtroom. I felt immediate peace, and that my life had just begun. My support system anxiously waited and anticipated a mood of utter desolation. I smiled when I saw them, grateful for their presence.

My baby sister, surprised, said, "I've never seen anyone look so happy after a divorce."

The truth is, I was all cried-out from years of trying to make a one-sided commitment work that ultimately chipped away at my soul. I was now liberated and felt full of possibilities.

The decision to leave was the hardest thing I've ever done. It took a lot of prayer, counseling, and ultimately self-love, to let go. The marriage had been on life support for years, with no potential to survive and thrive into a beautiful future. Removing myself from the toxicity was imperative to my destiny. There were several events that led to the courtroom, but there was one that rocked me to my core, and a clear indicator it was over.

Netflix and dinner alone had been a typical evening for me. The frequented movie category was romance; it gave me a sense of false hope, that maybe one day I would feel the love and adoration

I so desired. Watching a good film was a source of inspiration to write, and a distraction to shift the focus from my reality. Hours would pass, and I was happy that I was disciplined enough to work on my screenplay, but sad, I spent another night alone.

One night, the front door opened. In walked the man I was married to but felt like I didn't know anymore. I smiled and greeted him.

"Late rehearsal?" I asked.

He nodded.

I attempted to have a conversation, but he wasn't present, and I was soon cut off. He said that he needed a minute and begun to head upstairs. I noticed his ring finger was bare and I inquired.

"I left it on the bathroom sink." He replied.

My intuition told me otherwise.

Scared and hurt by what this could mean, I stayed up all night thinking. I became wearier over the relationship, and the distance between us had grown so much. My religious convictions prompt me to stay, but in my gut, I knew something was off. *I was supposed to forgive and take the disrespect*, and I couldn't leave unless I had absolute proof of infidelity, right? So, I constantly minimized the emotional abuse and *manipulation*. I was often stonewalled, and his behavior was always suspicious, placing me on a constant roller coaster. He had the control and loved it, and *my light slowly diminished.*

Desperate, I rushed us back into counseling, as if we were a maligned spine that needed a quick chiropractic fix. Soon after that, we were on an upswing and even talked about moving to California to pursue our dreams. We packed up our townhouse and planned to stay with family for a couple of months to save money. While packing at night, he helped me lad the last box that could fit into my car and said he would be right behind me. *He never showed up!*

I worried for four days before he finally called to say,

"I think we should separate."

I had so many emotions at that moment but remained stoic on the phone. I was furious and felt stripped of the vision I had for us. My anger turned into sadness. My heart literally crumbled. The man I loved and made a vow to in front of my family and to God didn't want me anymore.

I felt abandoned and rejected, and even questioned if there was something wrong with me. I felt unlovable. I cried for two weeks straight on my way to work and had to buy Visine so that no one would notice. *I hide my emotions; I couldn't bear to see the look of pity on people's face.* I withdrew from everything; all I could bring myself to do was work and lay in bed. I started to have chest pains, so severe I needed to go to the hospital to have an EKG test. I was diagnosed with having an anxiety attack, from all the stress I was experiencing. I was in a dark place and felt like I didn't want to live. I was ashamed and embarrassed and wished I could disappear.

As time passed, I started to feel better and came to grips with my new reality. When out of the blue, he called with his tail between his legs, apologizing. Naively, I took him back, but soon realized I couldn't live my life in a constant state of uncertainty of if he wanted to remain married. I vacillated for months on my decision to let go. After having a conversation with a family member, I had an ah-ha moment.

They said, "You know what? Ten years looks like here. You don't know what it looks like somewhere else, but are you willing to spend another ten years like this?"

A few days later, I had the conversation with him, with small hopes he would fight for me, but he looked relieved and wanted out. *I allowed myself to grieve, and learned healing comes in waves.*

I reclaimed my power and found inspiration in my pain. My creativity returned, I was stronger and felt more beautiful than ever.

I redirected my focus on moving to California to pursue my dream as a writer. I was excited about new beginnings, scared of the unknown, and sad that the life I once knew, no longer existed. However, I was ready to take flight to my destiny.

I hugged my family tightly and said my goodbyes and boarded the plane with a one-way ticket. During takeoff, I felt overjoyed and proud that I had chosen myself. I was happy I had finally made it onto California soil.

Reflection:

What decision are you currently vacillating about, and how can it delay your purpose?

CHAPTER 26

WHO AM I?
BY QUINN THOMPSON

The question of identity seems like it can be answered so easily, but, it is such a loaded question that requires much thought, and maybe even a bit of research. You'll be liberated when discovering who you really are! Most offenders struggle with self-identity, which can be one of the root causes of them repeating the cycle of abuse.

Most of them say, "That's just who I am."

However, that is an untrue statement. I raised that very question to my offender.

My exact words were, "The only way to get through it, is to stay before God. Go beyond yourself, and find out who you are…"

This is a turning point for both the victim and the offender. I had an assignment on self-identification from my mentor that had my mind churning for weeks. I thought I knew who I was, but to my surprise, I didn't! I mean, I knew whose I was, but didn't really know who I was. Sure, I told myself that I was a mom, a wife, an accountant for a major corporation, a preacher's daughter, lover of Christ, and so on. But this didn't tell me anything about myself. These were only a few titles that I'd came to possess over time. *They had nothing to do with the root of my heart, or character.* I had to study who I was, and the best way to do that was to ask God to reveal and reintroduce me to myself. To my surprise, when God answered that prayer, I felt a sense of freedom.

Offenders and victims of domestic abuse often suffer from an identity crisis. The victim sometimes feels that the offense was their fault because they did something wrong, so they tend to temporarily change their identity by altering their behavior or actions for a while until the offense is repeated. Oftentimes, the victim becomes confused because the change they made yielded no positive results. The cycle of confusion continues as she or he makes another temporary change in identity, because of identity uncertainty.

The offender is often a repeat offender due to the same reason. They seek anger management counseling to change their behavior and become a better person, but often revert to the same place they started because no real change occurred in their heart. The offender, and sometimes the victim, are both better at afflicting pain than managing it.

Yes, victims afflict pain by getting angry and wanting to avenge themselves by fighting back. *Anger management can't cure a matter of the heart*. Anger management therapy is a great tool to use, but as the title says, it only "manages" anger. Therapy teaches you how to live with the emotion. Only God can permanently change this behavior, and it starts in the heart, that identifies who you really are.

The heart affects vision, so if things are buried in your heart, it is impossible to see or think clearly. This is what the victim and the offender must realize. Therefore, prayer and faith are pertinent in domestic situations for both parties. God's Word says that we must walk by faith, and not by sight. (2 Corinthians 5:7).

As children, we are raised by parents who shape our morality, help develop our character, and we're sent into the world with our parent's perspective on life, not God's. This can cause issues down the road because the child is sent into the world with unrealistic expectations of how life is supposed to be. After a child leaves home, the world then begins to tell him or her who to be as an adult, thus causing the child to further deviate from who God says that he or she is.

I begin to think about Moses and how he suffered from an identity crisis. He had a choice to make. Am I Hebrew, or Egyptian? Being Hebrew would mean a life of suffering as a slave, along with humiliation and shame, whereas being Egyptian would yield a better life as Pharaoh's successor with much wealth and fame.

He chose to claim the identity God gave him and suffer with His people. Yes, it cost him some pain, but look at how he was liberated, and redeemed by God. Moses didn't deviate from who God said he was, and he was one of the most powerful men in the Bible! When God reveals to you who you really are, you are unlikely to deviate from it. Yes, it is uncomfortable to hear people speak their opinions about how the single victim helped their offender become a better person, or how the married victim decided to stick it out with their spouse after a domestic dispute but tune out the noise of the spectators. You now have a powerful testimony that will make unbelievers have a change of heart toward God, and possibly help someone who's silently crying for help with their domestic abuse.

Self-identification through God yields effective changes that some unbelievers will struggle to understand, but never let that discourage you. Don't allow the judgment of other individuals have such an impact on your healing process that it causes you to regress into thinking that doing what is right is ridiculous. It will disrupt any chances of God being able to step in and rescue you from the pain you are suffering from domestic abuse. Growth will only occur when you're willing to make a change. Change occurs in the heart that genuinely reveals who you are. Being who you're not will cause you to become overly exhausted while repeating cycles of abuse because real change has not occurred.

God will not bless who you pretend to be! I understand that change can be uncomfortable. It was difficult for me to change the trajectory of my life because I felt like I was doing all the right things, but I was getting nowhere. I had to realize what God was doing. I was in the growing process, and anything that grows becomes uncomfortable. I was turning a new leaf in my life, and *I thanked God for putting me in an uncomfortable place for growth to occur.*

- It's time to evaluate yourself. How do you treat your loved one(s) when no one is around versus when others surround you?
- What causes you to have a sense of insecurity about yourself to where you feel the urge to present yourself differently?
- Are you ashamed to be yourself around certain individuals due to fear of judgment?
- Do you find yourself being defensive when someone points out your vulnerability?

These are just a few questions to get you on the road to discovering *Y-o-u*. Most times, offenders and victims find that the roots of their issues lie deep within. It could be some detail of their past that they've just swept under the rug in efforts to forget about it, but it always tends to show up eventually, through their behavior and attitude toward others.

Did you know that Jesus can help you determine your identity through various scriptures in the Bible? He says that we are heirs of Christ and co-heirs of God in Romans 8:17, and that we are loved with an everlasting love in Jeremiah 31:3. In 2 Corinthians

5:20, He lets us know that we are His ambassadors, and that we have a secured future with Him in Jeremiah 29:11.

Never be afraid to be yourself. God purposely made you different, so that you can be set apart from others (1 Peter 2:9).

Reflection:

So, who are you? Take the challenge of self-identification, make the necessary changes, and live an abundant life of purpose.

CHAPTER 27

FLIP THE PAGE!
BY EMEM WASHINGTON

Dear Sister, *You*, are a woman of purpose. God has a purpose for your life. Those experiences you've had, the good and the bad, which have caused you to question whether God is with you, whether He sees you, or whether He hears you…they were for a purpose. I know this might sound cliché, but it is true. If you have had a miscarriage of the big dreams you once had, I am here to remind you that *Your story is not over*! I share my story with you, not because I enjoy talking about myself. But if there is an uplifting purpose in sharing my story, I will gladly share it.

Several years ago, a few months into my (first) marriage, I woke up in the worst pain I had ever felt. The pain was coming in waves. I went to the bathroom and discovered that I was bleeding. My (then) husband drove me to the hospital. Tests were done, and the pain was relieved, but the bleeding did not stop. A few hours later, we were told that we had lost our baby. It was called a stillbirth, because I was about 26 or so weeks into the pregnancy, past the first trimester. We were also told that I had uterine fibroids. We were asked if we wanted to see the baby and give him a name. What a tough question to answer! We decided to see the baby, and he looked perfect, except that he was smaller than my hand. We were told that it was nothing to worry about, that these things happen to many people.

Regarding the fibroids diagnosis, I wasn't that worried. My mom had experienced fibroids and had gone on to have all three of her children without having them removed. In fact, she did not have them removed until I was an adult (she had a hysterectomy). I knew that I would try again, with the fibroids in place. And I was not scared that I would have another miscarriage experience.

My next two pregnancies were lost at around 12 weeks and the fourth pregnancy lost around 26 or 27 weeks (like my first pregnancy). After I had lost my fourth child, the doctor told me that this would continue to happen if I did not have the fibroids removed. Although I had prayed and believed that my outcome would be somewhat like my mom's, I began to realize that my outcome would be different. So, I decided to have the fibroids removed. I found a specialist, and we set a date. When I awakened from surgery, the doctor came in to see me and gave me news which devastated me. Unfortunately, part of my fallopian tubes had been removed while removing the fibroids and I would not be able to get pregnant again, except via IVF (in vitro fertilization). I wept!! Sure, I had lost four children in a row, but at least, I had been able to *get pregnant* up until that time. Now it would require IVF. Where would the money for that come from?

But God! God is a faithful God. Even while trying to come up with the money for the IVF procedure, I kept praying and believing. I read stories of countless women (several in the Bible) who had had supernatural childbirths, and I began to claim the same for myself. About two months later, even though the Doctor had said it would not happen without medical help, I was pregnant!

I went on to have my first son the next year. I was ecstatic, and I was content. The rhythm of my new life as a mom was perfect. Sleepless nights were welcomed because I had my miracle and he was worth it.

When my son was a little over a year old, I began to think about a sibling for him. I was fine with one child, but I thought he might want someone to play with. However, I didn't want to appear ungrateful by asking God for too much, after all, He had given me this precious miracle. But I eventually expressed my desire for a sibling for my son. And God in His mercy granted my heart's desire. I initially wanted a girl, but when the Doctor told me it would be another son, I was very happy.

I share this because, even if you have never experienced a miscarriage (I pray you never do), you might find yourself in a situation where the dream you were carrying…your "baby," has come to an end. Maybe you have experienced the end of a marriage, or maybe the death of a loved one, or the loss of a job or house.

I can't tell you how your story will end, but please allow me to encourage you to believe that your story is not over. *Flip the Page* (and keep flipping if you must); your story is far from over.

Because of my miscarriage experience, I have been able to encourage others who are experiencing loss. If I had not experienced those miscarriages, I might have never been as convinced as I am to be able to tell others to hold on to their God-given dreams. Obviously, your story endings will vary. For me, God gave me children that I birthed, but before that, I reached a point where I knew that if He did not, I would be *okay*. For someone else, He may open the door for adoption. For another, He might allow childbirth through IVF or surrogacy. Or, He might cause another to realize that she can live a rich and fulfilling life without children of her own, but by sowing into the lives of orphans, or other people's children.

However, God chooses to handle it, rest assured that the loss that you have experienced is not the end of your story.

Reflection:

How will you flip the page?

CHAPTER 28

REBECCA AT THE WELL: SHOULD SHE WATER OR DOPPLER THE DROMEDARIES?
BY DR. MICHELLE K. WATSON

Moxie. Motivated. Mesopotamian. Matriarch. Multiparous. Manipulative. Malevolent. Mensch. Meshuganah. Maverick…

The alliteratives are aptly pertinent in the description of one of the most revered matriarchs of the Bible, Rebecca. For centuries, Rebecca has captivated the imaginations of the aristocratic scholarly and plebeian unlettered alike fundamentally due to her audacious introduction and her determinedly resolute disposition in charting the course of her destiny. In an era when women were defined primarily by their adroitness at home and hearth and robust fecundity, Rebecca is irrefutably an anomaly.

In the Book of Genesis, Rebecca cuts a supernatural, enigmatic figure; demonstrating her willing hand for industry by the seemingly effortless performance of a herculean task unbefitting a physically striking, intrepid young woman of means. Rebecca's experience at the well of *Araam-naharaim* is highly analogous to my own, after embarking upon a career in medicine. I quickly learned that to become a surgeon requires manual dexterity, mental acuity, and physical fortitude in an unrelenting operative atmosphere.

Surgeons are intimately familiar with the mastery of human fluid resuscitation. Regarding Biblical hidden figures to water a herd of ten dromedaries is not a feat for the faint of heart.

Under extreme desert conditions, and with an intricate series of physiological vascular adaptations, the Camelus dromedarius can survive severe dehydration and lose forty percent of body weight in water. To replenish this, and despite losing only 1.3 liters of fluid daily, the average 600 kg camel can drink 200 liters of water in under five minutes. One woman, ten camels, 2,000 liters per five minutes, and hours of labor makes this scenario seem very surgical.

Following toil, there is a reward, and Rebecca skillfully navigates the androcentric world of betrothal negotiations. In true celebratory fashion, the former mistress of the well bids the reader a *Departures* Magazine worthy Bedouin-style adieu; swathed in gold, and laden with the accouterment of a young woman who has arrived not by the precious metal utensil in her mouth, but through elbow grease and sheer grit! After the successful completion of my medical education, I can most assuredly relate to Rebecca. Shuck the gold shekel; I want Doppler ultrasonography and a scalpel.

As a vascular surgeon or a veterinarian, Rebecca could have applied Doppler sonography alongside her *beast mode* work ethic to build her own practice. A woman who operates, or who writes code as a computer scientist, or as a biomedical engineer who amplifies DNA, is highly unlikely to water a dromedary to win a man's favor. Her primary occupation is to water her own. *I chose to be that woman, but not without substantial opposition.*

When a dean enlightened me that I would never be "allowed" to become a surgeon, particularly due to my race; and how she would personally exercise her authority to prevent me from doing so, I took a deep breath, a long draught of well water, and tightened my fingers around my Doppler probe. Imagine the intensity of my anger with her oppressive, racist, divisive, and limiting ideology!

When Caucasian obstetrics professors shut the operating room doors in my face, telling me to stay out because I didn't belong there; while allowing my Caucasian classmates to enter freely, I was no longer thirsty for well water. I picked up my textbooks and studied as diligently as I could, while cradling my Doppler device for comfort.

When another physician and a resident secretly gathered my Caucasian classmates, and instructed them to meet in a private hospital area where they would exclusively dispense "special, privileged notes and education," I sighed.

In exasperation, I went to the library to study. I drank some well water and stared hopelessly at my Doppler.

When another dean publicly referred to me as garbage for desiring to train as a surgeon when I was not the descendant of a gilded surgical lineage, I nearly hurled my glass of well water *and* my Doppler at him! He later issued an apology, stating he had been ordered to ensure my becoming discouraged and exiting academia in order to maintain his position.

When a scientist informed me she had never sponsored an African-American in her laboratory for a Ph.D., because she believed, "The blacks were not willing to dedicate a lengthy number of years to advancing medical research science. Blacks prefer shorter study and fast money to purchase houses and cars for themselves and their parents," I was beyond *livid*!

Apparently, this woman was entirely unfamiliar with the brilliance of George Washington Carver, an agricultural chemist, botanist, and educator of international renown. Carver's innovative discovery of over 300 uses for peanuts led to one peanut product being used in the treatment of thousands afflicted with polio.

It is widely known that Dr. Mae C. Jemison, engineer, physician, astronaut, and scientist, was the first African- American woman to conduct experiments in outer space aboard NASA's spaceship Endeavour. Unfortunately, ignorance can indeed be bliss. The means in no way justify the ends. Their primitive behavior was detrimental, for it made me fight harder for my education. There is no feeling more incomparable than succeeding in an environment specifically engineered for the aerodynamic soundness of your failure.

The well serves as an allegory for an infinitesimal, copious, and bottomless reservoir of a divine wealth of primordial feminine wisdom; both boundless and limitless: without boundaries, sin barreras, sans frontiers. Rachel, Hannah, Esther, Mary, Dinah, Tamar, Sarah, Elizabeth, Leah, and Abigail, all drank here. When Rebecca refreshed the dromedaries, she selflessly gave of her essence to be restorative to others. This is what physicians like myself do.

Whose daughter are you?

Move forward, creating a multitude of job descriptions with as many hyphens as possible. Forge your future with una cualidad rebelde, a rebellious streak. Always have your mad money, and carry a Doppler in your purse. Like Rebecca, you are at the well to raise heck. #Beastmode

Reflection:

The evolution of Rebecca from a plucky and resourceful ingénue to a duplicitous, autocratic matriarch who worshipped at the altar of manipulation to unequivocally achieve the desired outcome is a topic long relished by Biblical scholars.

REBECCA AT THE WELL: SHOULD SHE WATER OR DOPPLER THE DOMEDARIES?

The Janus-faced duality of Rebecca's inherent character thoroughly resonates with many female trailblazers steadfastly forging career paths for themselves in the traditionally male-dominated fields of science, technology, engineering, and mathematics (STEM).

To ardently display Rebecca's willingness to aid, care for, and fulfill the needs of others is accepted as an undisputedly admirable feminine quality worthy of praise. However, for a woman to emulate the forwardness required by Rebecca to openly approach and successfully negotiate with masculine counterparts on her own terms, will almost always elicit varying levels of consternation in her milieu. In such an environment, men are rewarded for being brash and daring, with a smattering of devil-may-care bravado thrown in for good measure.

On the other hand, a woman's prowess to perform with an extraordinary proficiency, to advocate for herself in a room full of men, and to be a consummate professional always to win the right to be taken seriously, can lead her to face disparagement, ridicule, revulsion, and expulsion.

Oftentimes, female executives and employees bemoan the fact that men often finish their sentences for them or loudly speak over them as they are expressing themselves during boardroom meetings as if their opinions do not matter.

Au contraire, but they do.

Therefore, it is not enough for ladies to scream out of some random window that they are mad as heck and are not going to take it anymore. It is imperative that much like Rebecca, women go deep within to extract strength from their wells to act against social inequalities!

- What does your well look like?

- What have you had to do to receive acknowledgment in your career and to win the right to be taken seriously?
- What pearls of wisdom gleaned from your experiences would you offer to other women and impressionable young girls?
- What is your plan of action to take a stand against domination, control, and injustice?

CHAPTER 29

BREAKING DOWN BARRIERS
BY DR. PAMELA R. WIGGINS

Persistent, driven, and focused entrepreneurs look for ways to overcome and prevent obstacles!

Success Tip- "Begin with your destiny in mind."

I envisioned becoming a university professor, securing a university deanship, eventually writing a book, and becoming a business owner. What is your vision? After earning my bachelor's degree, I began my career in the social services field as a case manager working years with children and their families. Determined to make life better for my clients through education and awareness, I took an interest in teaching.

Success Tip- "The only opportunity you miss out on is the one you don't pursue."

I applied for a Field Trainer position to teach social services staff what I had spent so many years in the field practicing. I was interviewed and hired as a Field Trainer to provide relevant field practices to social services staff, as well as community service providers. I recall that even though I had great experience and the required education, I earned less than most of my colleagues. I was a bit disappointed at first, but soon realized that I could not get discouraged. Despite my hard work, I earned raises, but my salary never matched my colleagues.

After a few years of working as a Field Trainer, I decided to pursue my dreams of teaching at a local college or university while working full-time. I even thought about pursuing a deanship.

Success Tip- "Don't be discouraged; stay encouraged."

I began submitting applications to many local colleges and universities for teaching positions. It was discouraging sending out hundreds of teaching applications knowing I met the minimum qualifications; a master's degree in the subject area with 18+ hours to teach in the academic field.

After hundreds of applications and rejection letters stating something along the lines of, "Thank you for your application. After a careful search, we have selected another candidate who best meets our needs. We wish you the best of luck." I thought to myself, 'There is no such thing as luck; only unfailing prayer and faith in God to give me the desires of my heart.' After a long unsuccessful search, a local college contacted me to interview for an adjunct instructor teaching position; I was excited. I interviewed for the position and felt I interviewed well. I was later contacted by the dean of the college and offered an evening adjunct teaching position; I accepted the offer. I continued working full-time as a Field Trainer and would now pursue my dream of working part-time as an adjunct instructor.

Success Tip- "Patience and Persistence pays off."

I was teaching as an adjunct instructor for a little over one year when I learned the college associate dean of academic affairs was stepping down, and the position needed to be filled. I thought to myself; this is one of my dreams, so just go ahead and apply. At first, I had reservations about applying because I thought I was too young at the time. I had only been an adjunct instructor for a little over a year but had over three years of professional staff training experience. I applied for the associate dean of academic affairs position. After applying, I thought to myself, 'If I am hired, I will be working with an all-male Caucasian academic administration team. I would be the first African-American associate dean of academic affairs at the college.'

I was selected to interview for the position. I put on my best suit and prayed. I had a panel interview consisting of the all-male academic administration team, and the college president. I believed my interview went well. I was contacted and informed I was selected to be the next associate dean of academic affairs. At the age of 35, I became the first African-American associate dean of academic affairs at the college. I was so elated!

Success Tip- "Never underestimate your abilities."

After a short celebration, I transitioned into my new role, and yes, I still taught my evening classes. After a short time in my new position, I learned yet again, I was the lowest paid academic administrator. Not only was I the only female African-American academic administrator, but I was also the lowest paid academic administrator. What did this mean for me? It meant I was evaluating and leading academic administration who earned more than I did. I recall one of my staff, a department chair, came into my office, sat down, and put his feet up on my desk.

He said to me, "You know, if the shoe doesn't fit, you shouldn't wear it."

'Lord, help me; what do I say?' *thinking to myself.*

I politely responded, "I am glad that my shoes have always fit, and I have never had a problem wearing them."

I politely informed him that his behavior was unbecoming and would not be tolerated.

I later encountered this department chair sending out directives via email without my review and consent. I conducted counseling and informed him that his conduct was disrespectful, and was unacceptable. After this counseling, I had nothing but great support and compliance from this department chair.

Success Tip- "Remember to pray, stay the course, and allow God to fight your battles."

I enjoyed my deanship for several years. I was later hired at a university as an adjunct professor where nine years later, I am still employed and happy. I went on to pursue opening my staff training and consulting business which I thoroughly enjoy. Since opening my business, I have authored two books and began an unexpected career in public speaking.

Success Tip- "Do what you have to do now, so you can do what you want to do later."

Never give up. Trust God. Turn your dreams into reality. I did it, and you will too.

Reflection:

What obstacle can you overcome that may lead to an unexpected blessing in your life?

CHAPTER 30

BLOSSOMING INTO MY PURPOSE
BY ERIN WILLIAMS

My name is Erin Breaux Williams. I am 34 years old, and I live in Ponchatoula, Louisiana. Recently, I founded Femme a` Femme, a blog created to help women realize their power.

I am happily married to my husband, Shawn. We have three incredibly handsome and intelligent sons: Camron, 16; Shawn, 9, and Brenden, 6. Spending time with my family and writing inspirational content for my blog are two of my greatest enjoyments currently. Challenging myself and experiencing new adventures are other things I love to do. Although my life is ideal now, it was not always this way. I grew up in a two-parent home until the age of 12. Due to their love and encouragement, I progressed through high school and graduated a year early.

One month following my high school graduation, I discovered I was pregnant with my first child. At the time, I was 17, uncertain of my future, and how I would care for an infant. Nevertheless, I persevered with the support of my mother, child's father, and family. My family and I moved from the New Orleans, Louisiana area to Sugarland, Texas early on in my pregnancy. Once there, I enrolled in college. While uncertain of my future, I knew that education would be necessary for me to support myself and my child. My mother graciously offered to help me raise my son so that I could pursue my dream of college life on campus; the offer was truly appreciated. However, I decided to enroll in a nearby community college and completed my first semester of college with excellence. Shortly after the semester ended, I gave birth to my first son. I recall reading about the birth process and watching countless episodes of, *A Baby Story*.

None of what I read or saw fully prepared me for the immense joy and weight of the responsibility I experienced when I gave birth. Initially, I remember thinking that I couldn't wait until my life got back to normal. Eventually, it dawned on me that this was my new normal. Once my son was three months old, I resumed college courses at the same community college. I had to make more of an effort to get coursework done.

Thankfully, I had wonderful family support. My family and I moved back to the New Orleans area after I completed the summer semester. I accomplished several semesters of general studies and gained acceptance to Charity School of Nursing for the associate of science nursing curriculum.

Nursing school was one of the most challenging experiences I have ever had, but it was worth it. I completed nursing school as a registered nurse a few months after Hurricane Katrina. I was 21 when I started my first nursing job. A few months later, my son's father and I married. Our son was four at the time, and I was 22.

The hurdles I overcame to secure a future for my son and I contribute to the empathy I have not only for my patients but people as well. For several years, I practiced hospital-based nursing before venturing out to health plan nursing, where I currently practice. During that time, we added two more sons to our family, which made us a family of five.

Nursing is a rare field that has multiple levels to it. All levels of nursing have a purpose and positive contribution to society from the certified nursing assistant to the nurse with a doctoral degree. With ten years of nursing practice under my belt, I decided to return to college for a Bachelor of Science degree in nursing.

I decided to return to school to expand my options regarding career opportunities. I enrolled at Louisiana State University as an undergraduate nursing student in the curriculum designed for nurses who worked full-time.

In three semesters, I successfully completed the curriculum and earned a Bachelor of Science in nursing degree. Obtainment of this degree was a huge accomplishment for me; I felt proud of myself for returning to school after a 10-year break with a husband, three sons, and a full-time job. Once I earned this degree, I thought I was finished with education and had no need to return to school. However, a few years later, that changed.

Currently, I am enrolled at the University of South Alabama, in Mobile in an online program for graduate studies in nursing informatics. I will complete this curriculum summer, 2018. Getting back into the swing of things this time was not as difficult since I only had a 1 ½ year hiatus.

The pursuit of a graduate degree has added to my confidence level and empowered me to start Femme a` Femme blog. This blog was created with the intention of inspiring women to realize their own power. Women don't need to wait to be rescued by 'Prince Charming,' when we have the power to manifest our dreams by ourselves. I hope that every girl and woman who has a relationship with me or visits my blog, feels empowered to live life to the fullest on their terms, whatever that may be for them.

Each hurdle I overcame increased my self-worth and value, empowering me to have the confidence to set and achieve more goals. I also have a network of inspiring women whom I admire who are doing or have done things I want to do. *The power of influence is real!* Exposure to greatness and diversity gives one confidence to pursue one's dreams. In my short 34 years of life, I have grown so much, from being the teen mother who felt lost and confused to the empowered woman who wants to help more women pursue their goals. My life is not perfect, but it is mine. We cannot control everything that happens to us, but we can control our response.

Reflection:

What worries or fears do you have that keep you from becoming the person you hope to become?

CHAPTER 31

A ROSE FROM THE CONCRETE
BY DEBORAH YOUNG

It was a little after one o'clock in the morning as I sat locked away in the bathroom with a bruised eye, massive headache, and eyes full of tears. My husband and I had just finished having our eight hundredth argument over the course of our 3-year marriage that once again ended in a physical altercation. As a 20-year-old married woman, I could not understand why I thought marriage would be my happy ending. In fact, my marriage was filled with physical disputes, slow-healing bruises, sadness, anger, verbal attacks, countless tears, and lonely nights.

My life was a plane spiraling out of control, and there was no pilot to secure the landing. Sitting on the cold bathroom floor, I began to resent my horrible decisions: pregnant at eighteen, forfeiting my scholarship to a prestigious university, leaving my parent's home, were huge mistakes. I was embarrassed with how my life turned out. I gave up on all my dreams, *and I had no purpose.* Have you ever come to an extremely low point in your life? That night was my extreme low point.

I contemplated suicide but felt stupid afterwards, especially with my son sleeping in the next room. How selfish of me! My husband left after the argument, so I knew it was a perfect time to leave. If I moved quickly, I could catch the bus to my parent's house. I was too prideful to let my parents know about the abuse, so this would be a surprise to them. I packed a bag and left quietly. As I walked off the front porch, my husband appeared from the sidewalk. Suddenly, he pulled a gun from his jacket and demanded to know where I was going. I stood there speechless; I was so scared. Did he really intend to shoot our son and me? I couldn't take my eyes off the gun. I held our son tight, closed my eyes, and started crying.

Suddenly, a loud voice yelled, *"Put your finger on that trigger boy, and I will shoot you dead!"*

I opened my eyes to see our 70-year-old next door neighbor, a veteran and retired police officer pointing his gun directly at my husband. Realizing his mistake, my husband took off running, leaving me, our son, and the neighbor behind.

I knew I was given a second chance and I could no longer stay in the marriage. I moved back in with my parents, enrolled in nursing school, and started working. I devoted my time to my studies and my son. I also began partying and drinking excessively.

I was a mother and student during the day but an angry, violent, promiscuous, drunken party goer at night. Although I was trying to create a better life for myself, I was empty inside. Shortly after my divorce, I found myself in another relationship for four years that left me completely *heartbroken*. I became depressed and was unable to concentrate on my studies. As a result, I was dismissed from the nursing program in my senior year. To add salt to injury, I was laid off from my job the same week.

Why am I here?! I felt so lost. Four years passed since I walked away from my abusive marriage and my life was still filled with chaos and turmoil. In desperate need of some peace and clarity, I left Philadelphia and traveled to Houston to visit my sister. While in Houston, I visited Greater Works Ministries, a local church and non-profit organization founded by Bishop Shon Gray and his wife, Pastor Dena Gray. During altar call, I realized I needed a touch from Jesus. That is what I was missing! I created a life without Jesus, and *He is the One who reveals our purpose.*

That day, I received prayer. I do not remember the prayer that was prayed, but I remember Jesus' presence. I remember my pain, sadness, and heartache leaving me as an overwhelming feeling of love, peace, and comfort, overtook my heart. I never felt so much love at once. My journey with Christ began when Jesus visited me that day, and I am forever grateful for His presence.

From the day I received Jesus into my heart as my personal Lord and Savior and surrendered my life to Him, He revealed my purpose through my pain.

God has so much more in store for us than we have for ourselves (Jeremiah 29:11). I still remember my agony and the hopeless days that turned into sleepless nights. I hated myself for staying married for so long and subjecting my son to a hostile environment. The most difficult part of my journey was realizing that although I was in desperate need of love, I did not truly love myself. Why do we search for love but neglect loving ourselves?

I loved the "idea" of being in love, receiving affection, comfort, attention, and having someone to support and encourage me. I longed for appreciation and acceptance. My heart was in need, and I put pressure on a man to do a job I hadn't even taken on myself, to love me. In my efforts to find love, I had become the author of my own pain. All along, I had a Father in heaven who loves me unconditionally.

Roses take time to grow. They need soil, water, sunlight, and pruning. Pruning removes dead, damaged, and excess material from roses so that growth is not stunted. Gardeners find pruning roses to be a cumbersome and meticulous process but necessary.

Jesus pruned me despite my heartaches, horrible choices, and shortcomings. I am still amazed that true love like this really exists! The Lord healed and softened my stony heart. I am so undeserving yet grateful for His everlasting love. I want women around the world to be encouraged in knowing that true love *does exist*. Jesus is real, and He wants to heal, prune, and love you. A rose growing from the concrete is never heard of, but with Jesus, all things are possible.

Reflection:

Have you experienced the unconditional love of Christ that will propel you into your God-ordained purpose?

INDEX

A Baby Story, 142
A&T State University, 165
abandonment, 64, 84, 89
abortion, 46
abortions, 84
abuse, 23, 51, 121, 122, 123, 146, 162, 211
abusive, 49, 146, 211
academic life, 29
acceptance, 30, 83, 101, 142, 147
accusations, 37, 96
achievement, 50, 210
ACT, 30
activities, 29, 58, 183
Acts Full Gospel C.O.G.I.C., 181
adoption, 129, 196
adroitness, 131
Advil, 49
advocate, 12, 135, 162
afraid, 43, 46, 51, 63, 64, 65, 75, 77, 104, 113, 125
Agape, 97
altercation, 145
ambition, 38
ambitious, 27, 30
Anger management, 122
anger,, 13, 81, 95, 96, 145
animosity, 96
anointed, 59, 85, 111, 192
anointing, 22
anxiety, 13, 21, 30, 68, 81, 89
Anxiety, 13
Apostle Irene Huston, 181
apples, 17
appreciate, 27, 41
approval, 83, 88
Argosy University, 163

arguing, 12
Army Veteran, 30
ashamed, 59, 119, 124
assignment, 104, 111, 121, 200
atmosphere, 57, 111, 131
attitude, 57, 124
audacious, 131
audacity, 75
Austin Film Festival, 200
awakened, 111, 128
awards, 83
baby, 17, 45, 46, 47, 113, 117, 127, 129, 200
bachelor's degree, 137, 199
Bachelor's Degree, 50
backbite, 97
balanced, 42, 59
band, 32, 54, 105, 106, 107
Baruch College, 54
battles, 16, 21, 140
BCBG, 114
beast mode, 132
beautiful, 31, 47, 77, 79, 83, 84, 91, 117, 119, 185, 187, 196
beauty, 88, 179, 196, 211
Beauty for Ashes, 86
belief, 41, 165
believe, 26, 41, 43, 54, 57, 59, 65, 73, 82, 84, 90, 102, 129
Beloved, 23
Bethune-Cookman College, 93, 190
Bethune-Cookman University, 92, 190
Bible, 65, 96, 114, 123, 124, 128, 131, 181, 192
Bible Colleges, 181
Bible Study, 181
Biblical scholars, 134

149

INDEX

Bird of Paradise, 65
birthday, 46, 209
Bishop Bob Jackson, 181
Bishop T. D. Jakes, 73
Bishop T.D. Jakes, 182
bitterness, 96, 98, 99
Black Infant Health, 26, 189
bless, 22, 86, 124, 187
blog, 51, 111, 141, 143, 173, 197, 209
blossom, 84
blueprint, 23, 109
Boaz, 85
boldness, 38
bondage, 22
boulders, 117
Bowling Green State University, 171
brave, 53, 54, 55, 76, 77
breakthrough, 85
broken, 26, 36, 50, 69, 73, 85, 113, 146
brokenness, 60, 70, 84, 110, 187, 211
Bronx, 53
Burkina, 43, 171
burn out, 57, 58
business, 2, 17, 18, 27, 35, 46, 58, 66, 80, 90, 115, 137, 140, 164, 169, 176, 177, 185, 189, 199, 207, 211
caffeine, 17
California, 85, 118, 120, 166, 181, 192, 200
California State University, 166
calling, 15, 22, 32, 37, 38, 58, 59, 80, 88, 111, 187, 212
career, 12, 54, 83, 87, 92, 109, 115, 131, 135, 136, 137, 140, 143, 173, 177, 209
cast-away, 96
challenge, 43, 107, 113, 125, 169
Charity School of Nursing, 209
childbirth, 129
childcare, 114

children, 21, 22, 23, 45, 47, 67, 72, 79, 87, 122, 128, 129, 137, 164, 168, 172, 179, 183, 185, 192, 196, 203, 211
children's ministry, 168
choices, 13, 148
Christ, 31, 58, 61, 68, 85, 97, 121, 124, 147, 148, 181, 192, 211
Christian Universities, 181
Christmas, 16, 84, 89, 91
church, 31, 83, 96, 97, 110, 147, 165, 168, 181, 185, 203, 211
Cincinnati Playhouse, 200
clarinet, 105, 107
clarity, 111, 146
cohesive dysfunction, 37
college, 27, 29, 30, 32, 50, 54, 63, 79, 87, 88, 113, 138, 139, 141, 142, 143
collision, 69, 70
comfort, 17, 43, 60, 76, 147, 196
comfortability, 103
commitment, 55, 58, 117, 186, 190
community, 18, 30, 43, 55, 90, 114, 137, 142, 166, 174, 176, 185, 190, 194, 196
compassion, 36, 95, 192
complacency, 103
complacent, 31, 104
compromise, 26
concussion, 69
confidence, 43, 69, 143, 171, 211
confident, 19, 42, 43, 50, 77, 179
confusion, 22, 122
conquer, 22, 64
contagious, 72
control, 46, 51, 59, 63, 65, 66, 89, 94, 118, 136, 144, 145, 211
controlling, 26
Coral Gables, 91
cosmetology, 169
counseling, 117, 118, 122, 162, 197

INDEX

counterfeit, 85
courage, 43, 64, 65, 76, 77
create, 50, 57, 59, 90, 146, 165, 174, 179, 194, 197, 200
create change, 50
creative, 58, 85, 86, 169, 176, 188, 200, 203
creative writing, 176
crippled, 73
crossroad, 32
crowns, 83
crucified, 97
crying, 13, 36, 42, 84, 95, 123, 146, 192
cycle, 15, 22, 35, 121, 122
dark place, 18, 80, 119
date rape, 84
dating, 110, 111, 185
deanship, 137, 138, 140
debt, 87, 211
decide, 31, 32, 41, 59, 73, 75, 106, 200
Decide, 200
decisions, 77, 89, 109, 145
defeat, 22, 93
deliverance, 58, 84, 85, 192
Delta Sigma Theta Sorority, Inc., 190
Delta Sigma Theta Sorority, Inc.,, 190
demonized, 84
Department of Justice, 162
Departures Magazine, 132
DePaul University, 177
depression, 17, 21, 60, 88
Depression, 13
despair, 22, 109
desperate, 84, 146, 147, 187
destiny, 19, 22, 27, 74, 77, 101, 103, 104, 110, 115, 117, 120, 131, 137
determination, 27, 43, 205, 209
detours, 93, 111
die, 25, 68
dieting, 83
direction, 21, 22, 58, 72, 89

disagreement, 96
disappear, 114, 119
disappointment, 23
discipline, 65, 69, 205
disfigured, 71, 72
Disney World, 105, 106
disparagement, 135
Diversity, 190
divorce, 13, 64, 84, 111, 117, 146, 211
Doctorate of Education, 14, 163
Dollar General Store, 113
Domestic Violence Court, 92
Doppler, 132
Doula, 164
dream, 43, 59, 63, 85, 87, 88, 105, 106, 109, 120, 129, 138, 142, 165, 168
dream-chasers, 59
dreams, 43, 108, 118, 127, 129, 138, 140, 143, 144, 145, 164, 194
drinking, 36, 88, 146
dromedaries, 132
Dune, 63
Early Childhood Education Programs, 171
Ebola, 72
eczema creams, 18
educate,, 59
education, 11, 26, 54, 56, 132, 137, 142, 143, 166, 168, 169, 171, 192, 207, 209
effort, 17, 142
El Valle de Anton, 64
Elevation, 23
embarrassed, 145
emotional abuse, 22, 118
emotions, 13, 23, 42, 61, 64, 65, 119
empathy, 55, 142
employment, 12, 13, 47
empower, 55, 59, 174, 196, 203
empowered, 50, 143, 144
empowering, 12, 143

INDEX

empty-nesting, 79
encourage, 21, 43, 51, 59, 96, 111, 129, 147, 169, 174, 203
encouragement, 42, 141, 197
endurance, 57, 58, 59
endure, 21
engineering, 46, 135
enigmatic, 131
entertainment industry, 58
entrepreneurs, 137
envious, 97
environment, 23, 31, 135, 147
envy, 58
Epcot, 105
epiphany, 54, 109
Equal Opportunity Programs, 190
escape, 26, 54, 65, 194
Estee Lauder Laboratories, 205
evictions, 21
excellence, 2, 32, 142
exhausted, 37, 89
existed, 15, 17, 31, 120
existence, 58, 69
ex-offenders, 180
expenses, 30, 50
explore, 55
expulsion, 135
fail, 59, 61, 66, 102, 103
failing, 101
faith, ix, 21, 23, 24, 29, 32, 38, 57, 58, 60, 73, 75, 76, 79, 90, 93, 97, 115, 122, 138, 199, 214
faithful, 21, 57, 102, 115, 128, 211
family, 15, 17, 18, 23, 26, 30, 42, 45, 47, 51, 58, 65, 67, 68, 69, 71, 81, 84, 87, 89, 105, 113, 118, 119, 120, 141, 142, 162, 168, 177, 181, 196, 197, 200, 203, 207, 209
father, 11, 45, 47, 88, 107, 113, 114, 115, 141, 142, 209
favor, 81, 82, 87, 132

fear, 27, 30, 37, 38, 43, 54, 63, 64, 65, 66, 89, 101, 103, 104, 116, 124, 199, 211
Fear, 13, 63, 64, 65, 101
fearless, 53, 54, 55
Femme a` Femme, 141, 143, 209, 210
fibroids, 127, 128
finances, 115
financial, 13, 39, 105, 176, 211
financial stability, 13
First Lady Serita Jakes, 182
First-Aid, 72
fit in, 72
flaws, 74
Florida International University, 179, 190
forgiveness, 98, 99
Fortress, 23
foundation, 27, 168
freedom, 26, 77, 85, 122, 187, 211
Friedrich Nietzsche, 67
friends, 11, 15, 17, 18, 26, 31, 42, 49, 51, 53, 58, 79, 81, 85, 98, 105, 168, 169, 178, 196, 209
Functionally Depressed, 16
Gardeners, 148
generational, 22
gift, 29, 32, 33, 38, 56, 84, 110, 170, 196, 197
Girl, Just Color, 167
Girls Leadership Academy, 166
Global Christian Ministries, 181
Glut Food Co-Op, 47
goal, 43, 54, 106, 109, 169, 180, 192
Goal Digger, 167
goals, 43, 50, 54, 101, 144, 186
God, ix, 21, 22, 23, 26, 29, 31, 32, 38, 45, 47, 57, 58, 59, 61, 62, 65, 66, 68, 69, 70, 71, 73, 74, 75, 76, 77, 78, 80, 81, 83, 85, 86, 87, 89, 90, 93, 95, 96, 97, 98, 99, 102, 103,

INDEX

109, 110, 111, 112, 113, 115, 116, 119, 121, 122, 123, 124, 125, 127, 128, 129, 138, 140, 147, 148, 164, 165, 170, 181, 187, 192, 197, 201, 211
God's love, 21, 74, 77
God's will, 109
Golden Girls, 200
good enough, 41, 55, 64
good girl, 26
Gospel, 182
Gospel Rap, 59
gossip, 96
Governor, 91
Governor of Florida, Jeb Bush, 91
grace, 22, 23, 61, 62, 81, 87, 90
gracious, 95, 96
graduate, 64, 87, 88, 143, 190, 209
graduating, 32, 46, 58, 176, 181
Grammy Award Winning Artist, 58
Grammy Award Winning Producer, 74
grandmother, 47, 54, 81, 87, 179, 187
grateful, 77, 81, 114, 117, 147, 148, 164
Greater Works Ministries, 147, 211
green juice, 88
grill, 46
grounded, 18, 58, 77
guidance, 23, 30, 43, 58, 88, 111, 211
guilt, 84
gun, 146
Hampton University, 177
happiness, 13, 14, 47, 49
HBCU, 30, 54
heal, 27, 60, 71, 85, 110, 148, 192
healthy eating, 42
heart, 19, 22, 36, 38, 55, 57, 58, 59, 60, 61, 72, 75, 77, 83, 85, 88, 95, 96, 98, 109, 119, 121, 122, 123, 129, 132, 138, 146, 147, 148, 181, 192, 205, 209, 212
heartache, 27, 147

Heavenly Father, 23, 82, 95
hide, 71, 72, 77, 119
hiding, 26, 74
high school, 29, 30, 31, 32, 63, 87, 105, 141, 168, 209
Holidays, 87, 89
Holy Spirit, 69, 95, 96, 165, 192
Home Line', 18
homeless, 22
homeowner, 51
hope, 18, 21, 29, 59, 101, 117, 143, 144, 192, 203, 209, 211
hopeless, 50, 147
hospital, 68, 69, 88, 127, 142
Human Resource Management, 169
humble, 11, 21, 190, 192
Hurricane Katrina, 142
hurt, 16, 45, 49, 54, 55, 81, 98, 99, 118
husband, 12, 13, 32, 47, 84, 127, 141, 143, 145, 146, 200
hysterectomy, 128
identity, 37, 121, 122, 123, 124, 197, 212
iheartbrowngirl, 51, 173
Imagine, 181
immunity, 71
impatience, 58
Imperial Hair Designs, 211
in love, 26, 37, 65, 147, 164, 192, 200
infidelity, 84, 118
influence, 96, 144
inner-healing, 85
insecure, 42, 65
insecurities, 38, 50, 65
inspiration, 109, 118, 119, 166, 183
inspirational, 141, 192, 194, 203
insurance, 69, 173
integrity, 23, 32
intention, 74, 143
interaction, 41
internship, 114

INDEX

intimacy, 95, 96
Intrinsic Shift: Shifting and Winning in Life, 183
intuition, 110, 118
invisible, 68, 71
Isolation, 84
IVF, 128, 129
Jacksonville Theological Seminary, 179
Jacob Krueger Studio, 200
Jehovah Jireh, 23
Jerry Perzigian, 200
Jesus, 31, 62, 97, 99, 102, 124, 147, 148, 165, 181, 192
Jewish, 123
job, 18, 26, 27, 29, 30, 49, 50, 54, 63, 64, 79, 87, 88, 89, 107, 114, 115, 129, 142, 143, 146, 147, 164, 168
John Ehret High School, 209
John Maxwell, 190
Jonah, 38, 95, 96
journalism, 114
joy, 26, 45, 90, 108, 116, 142, 211
Jubilee Christian Center, 85, 181
Jubilee Christian Center Bible College, 181
Judge, 190, 191
Judge McWhorter, 190
judgement, 97, 110
judgment, 32, 123, 124
judgments, 41
Kaplan University, 189
Keion Henderson, 74
kindness, 95, 96
Kissed by Lenore, 18, 164
Lady Serita Jakes, 182
Land of the rising sun: A Fictional Tribute to Biafra, 194
leaders, 31, 56, 59, 166, 174
leaving, 12, 17, 45, 46, 54, 64, 72, 145, 146, 147, 190, 205
left-handed, 83

legalism, 85
legalistic, 83
lesion, 71
lesson, 27, 77, 114
lessons, 37, 93, 111, 183, 197
liberated, 117, 121, 123
life support, 117
Lincoln University, 54
Lions Group Financial Planning, 211
living water, 96
Living Word Church, 32
Livingston, 31, 32, 168
logic, 55
lonely, 50, 145
Lord, 2, 29, 31, 59, 60, 62, 67, 70, 84, 96, 97, 101, 139, 147, 148, 179, 181, 192
Lord Jesus Christ, 182
lose weight, 42
lost, 17, 23, 32, 36, 46, 53, 68, 79, 81, 89, 110, 115, 127, 128, 144, 146, 180, 192, 194
love, 17, 21, 25, 26, 27, 32, 35, 36, 37, 38, 39, 51, 55, 59, 64, 65, 69, 70, 77, 80, 84, 85, 87, 88, 90, 95, 96, 97, 98, 117, 124, 141, 147, 148, 169, 173, 183, 187, 189, 194, 197, 200, 211
Love's Legacy, 194
Loyola Marymount University, 189
M&M's, 35
maggots, 46
marathon, 57, 58
marathon,, 59
marked, 59, 71
marriage, 64, 75, 76, 85, 110, 117, 127, 129, 145, 146, 211
married, 32, 87, 109, 118, 119, 123, 141, 142, 145, 147, 168, 187, 204, 209
mask, 37, 38

INDEX

master's degree, 27, 138, 168, 199
Master's Degree, 54
mathematics, 135
Matriarch, 131
medicine, 49, 131, 205
meditate, 59, 61
MeDitation Nation, 206
mental, 23, 51, 55, 131, 162, 197, 211
mental health, 55, 162, 197
Mephibosheth, 73
merciful, 95, 96
Mexican immigrants, 83
Mickey Mouse, 105
military, 12, 13
millennials, 59
mind, 21, 26, 27, 37, 57, 59, 60, 63, 64, 65, 73, 75, 79, 81, 87, 98, 110, 121, 137
mindset, 29, 58, 59, 81
ministry, 22, 23, 98, 187, 192, 211
minorities, 59
mirror, 42, 84, 98
miscarriages, 129, 200
misery, 49, 98
mistakes, 60, 111, 145
molestations, 84
money, 16, 26, 30, 46, 47, 50, 54, 58, 106, 113, 118, 128
morals, 110
Moses, 123
mother, 11, 17, 27, 32, 45, 46, 54, 83, 85, 87, 102, 107, 113, 141, 142, 144, 146, 162, 169, 172, 179, 181, 185, 187, 192, 194, 196, 199, 204, 209
motherhood, 26, 27
motivate, 42
motivational speaker, 166, 173, 185, 207
Mount St. Joseph, 200

music, 73, 105, 106, 107, 108, 164, 165, 176, 182, 203
My Life Journal Bible Study Series, 181
National University, 163
negativity, 41, 98
neglect, 76, 147
Netflix, 117
new heart, 85
Nineveh, 95
No Chumps Allowed: 7 Keys to Activating your Inner Champion, 183
non-profit organization, 55, 147, 165
Nora's Organic Kitchen, 187
North Carolina, 45, 164, 165, 172
nourishment, 59, 110
Nova Southeastern University, 179, 207
NSU, 179
nurse, 73, 88, 142, 143, 194, 209
nursing, 142, 143, 146, 209
nursing school, 142, 146
nutritionist, 42
obstacles, 21, 51, 81, 137, 169, 173
offended, 98
offender, 121, 122, 123
offenses, 98
officers, 68, 69
olive skin, 83
opponent, 106, 107
opposition, 30, 132
oppression,, 21
optimism, 57
orphans, 129
outcast, 41
outspoken, 53, 54
overcome, 43, 51, 108, 137, 140, 169, 173, 183, 189, 211, 214
overcoming, 81, 173, 203
overprotective, 45

INDEX

pain, 16, 23, 36, 49, 54, 60, 61, 68, 70, 99, 111, 119, 122, 123, 127, 147, 211
Pampers, 113
Panama, 63, 64, 65, 66
Pandora, 164
parables, 102
parent, 27, 113, 122, 141, 146
Park University, 163
partying, 146
passport, 55, 174
peace, 31, 37, 49, 68, 79, 110, 117, 146, 211
Peace Corps, 171
peers, 29, 30
Pendio Enterprise, 183
Pepperdine University, 176
perfectionist, 84
perform, 83, 106, 135, 177
perspective, 22, 26, 39, 55, 81, 122, 174, 196
Pharisees, 97
philosophy, 2
plan, 13, 14, 29, 30, 74, 79, 87, 89, 106, 109, 110, 136, 142, 185
plans, 15, 26, 29, 38, 65, 69, 87, 101
plastic surgeon, 71
poetry, 169, 183, 197
Poised Polished Professional: The Experts' Guide for Executive Presence, 185
police, 146
possibilities, 117
potential, 66, 102, 117, 176, 203
power, 41, 47, 50, 51, 55, 65, 77, 96, 119, 141, 143, 144, 209
praise, 23, 47, 98, 135
pray, 57, 129, 140, 192
prayer, 59, 95, 102, 117, 122, 138, 147
prayer affirmations, 59
prayers, 68
praying, 31, 71, 97, 110, 128

preacher's daughter, 113, 121
pregnant, 26, 46, 47, 96, 113, 128, 141, 145, 200, 209
Pre-K Teacher, 168
pre-teen, 53
pretended, 15
pride, 58, 107
Prince of Peace, 60
prisoner, 98
process, 21, 23, 39, 43, 58, 77, 96, 101, 111, 123, 124, 142, 148, 187
professor, 137, 140, 162, 207
program, 27, 64, 85, 90, 143, 146, 166, 169, 180, 185
promiscuous, 11, 146
promises, 23, 65, 66, 102, 111
prophetic, 85, 97
prosperity, 59
proud, 17, 84, 120, 143, 187, 204
provision, 23
prowess, 135
Pruning, 147
public speaking, 140
Puerto Rico, 63
pump my stomach, 25
Purple Inked, 66, 177, 178
purpose, 2, ix, 12, 17, 18, 19, 22, 23, 35, 38, 39, 53, 55, 56, 58, 59, 60, 63, 66, 68, 69, 70, 72, 74, 75, 77, 80, 82, 86, 90, 96, 98, 101, 102, 103, 104, 109, 111, 115, 116, 120, 125, 127, 143, 145, 147, 148, 166, 169, 174, 181, 187, 197, 199, 202, 203, 211, 214, 217
purpose-driven life, 101
qualified, 89, 180
race, 57, 59, 60, 61, 62
rage, 11, 85
rainbows, 27
raw whole foods, 46
reap, 22, 116

INDEX

Rebecca, 131, 132, 134, 135
rebellious, 84
Rebirth, 203
rebuild, 50
recharge, 81, 169
red flags, 109
re-entry services, 162
reflection, 42, 77, 93, 214
registered nurse, 209
regret, 58, 60
regrets, 29
rejection, 64, 71, 72, 74, 101, 103, 138
relationship, 23, 31, 38, 49, 50, 77, 88, 90, 95, 99, 111, 115, 118, 143, 146, 173, 181, 185
relationships, 11, 32, 57, 99, 169, 173, 179, 185
religious, 97, 118
repossessions, 21
reputation, 97, 106, 205
resentful, 84
resiliency, 27
resilient, 53
resources, 22, 30, 50, 174
restoration, 111, 187
restore, 23, 93
revive, 93
risks, 29
romance, 117
sabotage, 84
sacrifice, 22
sacrificial, 97
sadness, 13, 119, 145, 147
Salvation Army, 115
sanity, 26
Sarcoidosis, 71
Savior, 147, 181
scalpel, 132
scholarship, 32, 145
science, 135, 142, 164
Science, 143, 163, 164, 173, 179, 189

Screencraft, 200
screenplay, 118
screenplays, 73, 177
scriptures, 59, 124
second chance, 70, 146
secrets, 84
self-awareness, 55
self-worth, 50, 143, 166
senior year, 29, 46, 146
setback, 23
shame, 58, 84, 115, 123
single parenting, 115
singleness, 11, 12, 14, 110, 111
slander, 96
sleep, 15, 25, 37, 68
Sloppy Joe's, 46
social media, 32, 111
Social Media, 18
social services, 137
society, 15, 143, 169, 179, 197, 209
songs, 73
sophomore, 105
sowing, 129
Spain, 43
Spelman College, 58, 176
spiral, 15
Spirit, 65, 95, 96
spiritual attack, 23
spiritual encounter, 23
spiritual gift, 33
sporting events, 105
Springfield Gardens High School, 179
sprinter, 57
Squad of Survivors, 166
St. James A.M.E. Zion, 165
Starbucks, 53
Statement Junky, 55, 174
STEM, 135, 164, 205
stigma, 55
Stimulation to Success Ministries, 165
stolen, 80

INDEX

storm, 27, 63
storms, 27
strength, 27, 37, 43, 52, 58, 59, 60, 67, 77, 210
stressed, 71
strict, 45
Strong Tower, 23
struggle, 17, 23, 58, 90, 121, 123
stubbornness, 58
student loans, 50
Suburban, 67, 68
success, 11, 12, 14, 58, 61, 103, 104, 168
Successful Reintegrations, 180
suicidal, 50
suicide, 21, 145
Summa Cum Laude, 93
support system, 117, 166
surgeon, 131, 132
surrogacy, 129
surrounded by love, 17
survivor., 11, 12
sympathy, 21, 42
teach, 21, 43, 102, 137, 138, 181
technology, 135
Ten Steps to Happy, 166
test, 30, 108
testimony, 21, 81, 111, 123, 197
tests, 21
Thanksgiving, 16
The 1812 Overture, 107
The Bishop's Choir, 165, 182
The City Beautiful, 91
The Dark-Skinned One, 83
The Fresh Prince of Bel-Air., 63
The Jeffersons, 200
The Lazarus Foundation, 211
The Man Who Fell in Love With Kimberly, 177
The Ohio State University, 197
The Passport Queen Project, 175

The Potter's House, 73, 165
The Potter's House Choir, 73
theJSbrand, 115, 199, 200
therapy, 51, 54, 55, 111, 122
Therapy, 122, 200
third day, 93
thirsty, 58
Thru Grace Media, 211
to Charity School of Nursing, 142
tongues, 97
torment, 84
Torn, 38, 169
tow yard, 69
toxic, 38, 115
toxicity, 35, 117
Trader Joe's, 72
tragedy, 27
trailblazers, 135
transformation, 110
transitioned, 15, 139
transparent, 21, 22, 55
transportation, 21, 30
traps, 103
trauma, 14, 54, 197
Travel, 55
treatment, 26, 97
trials, 11, 21
tribulations, 11, 14
triumph, 27
trophies, 83
true love, 148, 194
truth, 23, 38, 53, 77, 80, 82, 83, 85, 110, 117, 192
tuition, 50
turmoil, 14, 25, 146
Tuscaloosa County High School, 168
U.S. Postal Service, 46
ugly, 36, 38, 41, 83, 89
U-Haul, 37, 80
ultrasonography, 132
unbelief, 23

INDEX

unconditional, 85, 148
unconditionally, 17, 147
unemployment, 115
United States Marine Corps, 162
universities, 29, 30, 138
University of District of Columbia, 46
University of Florida College of Law, 93
University of Florida Law School, 190
University of North Carolina, 164
University of Phoenix, 165, 207
University of South Alabama, 143
University of West Alabama, 31, 168
unknown, 91, 120
unlovable, 119
uplifting, 12, 127, 194
UWA, 31, 32
vacation, 88
Vacation Bible School, 181
VCH Prosperity Consulting, 166, 167
vegan diet, 46
vegetarian, 47, 172
veteran, 12, 146
Veterans, 163
veterinarian, 132
victim, 51, 109, 116, 121, 122, 123, 162
victim services, 162
village, 18, 164

vision, 57, 58, 102, 104, 119, 122, 137
voice, 25, 27, 67, 75, 80, 91, 102, 146, 192, 203
Volunteering, 47
vulnerability, 55, 124
walking, 17, 21, 38, 53, 55, 72, 86, 98, 187
Washington, D.C., 45
waterfalls, 64
weight, 42, 43, 88, 89, 132, 142
What is This Thing Called Love, 169
When Dreams and Visions Collide, 194
whiplash, 68
Whitney Houston, 59
wholeness, 14, 111
Wiggins Management & Consulting, LLC, 207
witness, 23
worship, 57, 95, 203
worshipping, 69, 110
worthy, 49, 106, 132, 135
wreck, 68
write, 38, 57, 59, 66, 73, 102, 118, 197
Writer's Anonymous, 183
YWCA, 190
Zeta Phi Beta Sorority, Incorporated, 164

About the Authors

ABOUT THE AUTHORS

DR. NAJAH A. BARTON

Dr. Najah A. Barton is a native of Brooklyn, New York. Born in Guyana, South America, her mother relocated to the 'Big Apple' when Dr. Barton was five years old. She remained there until joining the Armed Forces in 2006. Since 2006, Dr. Barton has been a Federal government employee, working in the legal services, advocacy, and victim services fields—on active duty, and as a civil servant. As a victim services professional for over ten years, she has lent her professional and personal time to a host of pursuits. This includes serving as a victim's advocate, mental health counselor, professor, and a training facilitator. At this time, encompassed under her leadership in her role as a senior-level manager within the Department of Justice, Dr. Barton oversees specialized programming inclusive of mental health, victim services, and other sensitive care services. Prior to that, she served as the Victim Advocate Program Manager, Headquarters Marine Corps, United States Marine Corps. Dr. Barton served as the Marine Corps subject-matter expert (SME) for all victim services issues including but not limited to: compensation via the Transitional Compensation for Abused Family Members Program, child maltreatment, domestic abuse, policy writing for the Marine Corps, and other akin or co-related family/intimate partner violence matters. As a vibrant and driven professional, Dr. Barton is engaged and involved with many entities. She serves on the Board of Directors for a local non-profit agency in the state of Virginia, which focuses on re-entry services for returning citizens; provides unpaid mental health counseling services at two local non-profit healthcare organizations in Virginia, and has previously facilitated group(s) at several locations including at her local Department of Veterans Affairs in Washington, DC. Dr. Barton holds a Doctorate of Education in Counselor Education and Supervision from Argosy University, Northern Virginia; a Master of Arts in Forensic Psychology from Argosy University San Diego; a Master of Arts in Human Behavior from National University, and a Bachelor of Science in Criminal Justice Administration from Park University.

For inquiries, speaking engagements, book signings, and other special events contact:
Dr. Najah Barton
beingdrbarton@gmail.com
Website: Iamdrbarton.com
YouTube: Dr. Barton's Soap Box
LinkedIn: Dr. Najah A. Barton
Facebook: I Am Dr. Barton Business Page

ABOUT THE AUTHORS

Jazmine Blake

Jazmine Blake is an educator in North Carolina. Raised in Durham, NC (Bull City), she attended the University of North Carolina at Greensboro where she graduated with a degree in English and joined the Illustrious Zeta Phi Beta Sorority, Incorporated. God smiled on her when He blessed her with a job, teaching Science in the area. Ever since, she has been dedicated to helping students across the state fall in love with various aspects of the science field. She even began a STEM summer camp to serve children in the area. While working as a nomadic educator, she has taught nearly 1,000 students how to be better students as well as how to be better people. When Jazmine is not working with children, she can be found reading Romance and Young Adult novels on her porch with her Great Aunt, Celia, and her German Shepard, Zoe. A lover of music, her Pandora will play anything from rhythm and blues to classical, to gospel, or even country depending on the day and the distance she has to drive. Jazmine spends the rest of her free time with her brothers Asa, JaRon, and Brian, supporting them in their dreams. She is grateful for her village and Sister-Friends that keep her going. She currently runs a self-care business, Kissed by Lenore, and is taking classes to become a Doula.

For inquiries, speaking engagements, and book signings go to www.smarturl.it/jzblake.

ABOUT THE AUTHORS

Vanessa Brown

Minister Vanessa Brown was born in Lincolnton, North Carolina. She accepted Jesus at the age of 12 at an established local church, St. James A.M.E. Zion. Not having a youth choir, she joined the adult choir at 12. She received the Holy Spirit at age 18.

Vanessa graduated from Lincolnton High School in North Carolina, in 1994. She went on to receive a bachelor's degree in Professional English (Arts) from North Carolina A&T State University, in Greensboro, NC, in 1998. And later relocated to Texas in 2006 and received her master's degree in Information Systems from the University of Phoenix in 2013. From 2006 to 2013 she gained a broad knowledge of technical writing and the music industry. Vanessa is the Founder of Stimulation to Success Ministries, a non-profit organization, since 2015. Stimulation to Success Ministries was formed out of the belief that all people can develop and create a healthy and effective life regardless of how difficult or painful their day-to-day pressures, challenges, and struggles. Currently, Minister Brown is a member of The Potter's House Church, in Dallas, Texas, founded by Bishop T. D. Jakes. She serves in The Bishop's Choir, under the tutelage of Dr. Valerie Crumpton. As a catalyst to her dream of doing everything 'Large in God' and for GOD, Vanessa actively serves God and the Let the Light Shine: A New Gospel Project, as well as Shine the Light Network.

For inquiries, speaking engagements, book signings and other special events go to www.smarturl.it/vbrown.

ABOUT THE AUTHORS

VERONICA CLANTON-HIGGINS

Veronica Clanton-Higgins, MSW, is an author, an educator, a life coach, motivational speaker, and CEO of VCH Prosperity Consulting. A native of Compton, CA. Veronica is known for her community advocacy, support and healing of women, and youth mentorship. Veronica started VCH Prosperity Consulting in 2016 to address the social, emotional, and spiritual needs of women in her community. This was accomplished using workshops that focused on connecting women through sisterhood. Her unique style of Life Coaching is a combination of empowerment, motivation, and inspiration. She has made it her life's purpose to improve the lives of others by helping them discover their self-worth by using mindfulness and self-affirming techniques. Veronica promotes change through education. She created S.O.S. (Squad of Survivors), a nine-week program that promotes healing through the sisterhood collective. Veronica uses this method because "healing is more effective when you have a strong support system." She is also the founder of (The Girls Leadership Academy) for young women. T.G.L.A is a seven-month curriculum for middle school youth that encourages young women to focus on their strengths in order to be effective leaders in school and their neighborhood. Veronica's work also includes a research study in collaboration with California State University, Long Beach, that focuses on reducing stress in African-American women through the use of psychoeducation. During her free time, Veronica enjoys writing. Her works include a thought-processing journal, *Ten Steps to Happy*, a planner for women in direct sales, *Goal*

ABOUT THE AUTHORS

Digger: Planner for the Direct Sales Diva," and a stress reduction coloring book, *Girl, Just Color.*

For inquiries, speaking engagements, book signings, and other special events contact:
Veronica Clanton-Higgins, MSW
VCH Prosperity Consulting
hello@ prosperwithvch.com
www.prosperwithvch.com

ABOUT THE AUTHORS

ALEXANDRIA CUNNINGHAM

Alexandria Cunningham was born in Chattanooga, Tennessee and raised in Northport, Alabama, where she lived until the summer of 2010. She moved to Livingston, Alabama to further her education at the University of West Alabama. In 2015, she received a bachelor's in interdisciplinary studies and received her master's degree in education in May of 2018. As a child, she attended wonderful schools from kindergarten through high school. Tuscaloosa County High School professed a strong educational and ethical philosophy that has remained with her throughout her teaching. It is the foundation, along with the continued support of her family, educators, and friends that has allowed her to embrace her dream of teaching children. Through her collegiate years, she took on many clubs, organizations, and jobs. With each new club, organization or job, she learned time management, leadership skills, and visited many places. While in Livingston, she met the man that she would later marry. In 2016, Kirstan and A.J. married in Calera, Alabama, with a full attendance by family and friends. A.J. is a Pre-K Teacher and serves in the children's ministry at her church. She believes with the wonderful support of her loved ones and colleagues; she will become a teacher who young children look up to, someone children can trust, who will always 'go the extra mile' to ensure their success.

For inquiries, speaking engagements, and book signings go to smarturl.it/acunningham.

Nikeisha Darensburg

Nikeisha Darensburg was born in Washington, DC and has worked in many fields which include but are not limited to: education, program administration, and cosmetology. As a single mother, she embodies the definition of perseverance. A self-love enthusiast, she is on a continuous mission to overcome obstacles and embrace her purpose. Nikeisha has been a lifelong learner and is constantly seeking to grow and challenge herself in new ways. She is currently studying Human Resource Management and aspires to head her own business consulting firm for startup companies. Nikeisha has had a passion for writing for many years that first manifested itself in the form of poetry. Her first poem was entitled *What is This Thing Called Love?* She has written numerous works for both business and academic purposes. Nikeisha is currently working on a novel, *Torn*, that will be released in the future. Able to identify with the struggles and plight of women in society, Nikeisha seeks to encourage and equip women to learn self-love and strive for independence. Nikeisha's goal is to effect change through her writing. Nikeisha stands out as a writer because her stories are real, raw, and relatable. Her work is thought-provoking and emotional. Nikeisha's platform is based on many of the issues that women are dealing with: self-doubt, domestic violence, undefined purpose, lack of support, and personal relationships. When she isn't working or tackling a project, Nikeisha can typically be found with her daughters. Her home is full of laughter as she enjoys being surrounded by friends and those who rejuvenate her spirit. Nikeisha equally values her solitude that she uses to recharge and allow her creative thoughts to flow.

ABOUT THE AUTHORS

Recognizing her writing as a God-given gift, Nikeisha has come to realize the importance of operating in purpose through her gift of story-telling.

For inquiries, speaking engagements, book signings, and other special events contact:
Nikeisha-nicol@hotmail.com
PH: 410.831.8551

ABOUT THE AUTHORS

BENTA DAVIS

Benta Davis has a B.A. in International Studies with a focus on Communications from Bowling Green State University. After graduation, she was accepted in the Peace Corps in 2014 as an Education Volunteer in Burkina Faso, West Africa, where she lived for two years, developing Early Childhood Education Programs, and working with over young girls on the importance of education, reproductive health, self-confidence, and leadership. After participating in the Peace Corps, Benta returned to Washington, DC., where she is now working in the field of International Public Health.

For inquiries, speaking engagements, book signings, and other special events go to www.smarturl.it/bdavis.

ABOUT THE AUTHORS

JUDY DAVIS

Judy Davis is the seventeenth child born to Sallie Moore and Nelson Davis on March 8, 1954, in Wilson, NC. Judy is a Natural Health and Beauty Consultant at one of the oldest natural food, non-profit Cooperatives in the country. She is also a vegetarian and a mother of nine children.

For inquiries, speaking engagements, book signings, and other special events contact:
Judy Davis
1641 West Virginia Ave NE
Washington, DC 20002

ABOUT THE AUTHORS

Chontae Edison

Chontae Edison is 32-years-old and currently resides in Georgia. She picked up the love for writing when she was around the age of nine. Chontae never thought about writing professionally until later on in life when she was dealt her own obstacle. In overcoming the challenges of an unhealthy relationship, she realized other women could benefit from her journey and experience. Upon this realization, she began iheartbrowngirl, a blog where women can read about her experiences and hopefully feel compelled to share their own. While balancing a blog, she has a full-time career in the insurance industry and currently holds a Bachelor of Science Degree. She is also a motivational speaker and helps other women overcome their obstacles specifically in unhealthy relationships.

For inquiries, speaking engagements, book signings, and other special events contact:
PH: 631.747.5436
iheartbrowngirl.com
iheartbrowngirl@gmail.com

ABOUT THE AUTHORS

RASHELL EVANS

Rashell Victoria Evans is a native New Yorker who currently resides in Westchester County. She is the Founder and Executive Director of Statement Junky, a not-for-profit organization dedicated to gifting minority girls with an essential key to access the world—their first passport. Rashell started Statement Junky in 2017 because she believes the future depends on a new breed of leaders, ready to solve the world's problems. Passion and purpose will only take girls so far. Leaders need the right mix of values, skills and worldly experiences. Before devoting her work to Statement Junky, Rashell served as the Director of Operations for a leading High School in Harlem, New York. Her leadership and rapport with parents and students afforded her the opportunity to chaperone 25 teenagers to Quito, Ecuador, for a service-learning trip. Rashell coins the trip to Ecuador as the international experience that changed her global perspective and inspired her to create travel opportunities via the gifting of passports to young women across the nation. Since then, Rashell has equally explored the globe, most recently, landing her in Australia where she was able to take a selfie with a Kangaroo. Currently, Statement Junky has awarded over a dozen young women with their first passport. With each passport, a young woman has up to 10 years of no excuses to travel the world and change the world. Rashell's website StatementJunky.com, online community, and mentorship, are designed to empower, encourage and inspire young women to travel internationally with access to other travelers and resources necessary for exploration.

ABOUT THE AUTHORS

Rashell is excited about her next endeavor, a youthful travel enterprise designed to ignite the travel experience for young women starting in the classroom. Stay tuned, *The Passport Queen Project* is coming soon.

For inquiries, speaking engagements, book signings, and other special events contact:
Rashell Evans
PH: 347.913.5354
StatementJunkyInfo@gmail.com
StatementJunky.com

ABOUT THE AUTHORS

INCREDIBLE FAITH

Incredible Faith currently resides in Dallas, Texas. After graduating from Spelman College with a bachelor's in economics & also obtaining a master's in management & leadership from Pepperdine University — Graziadio School of Business, she started a creative financial firm, *Lead.Love.Save.Serve., LLC* in order to serve small businesses, nonprofits, churches and the greater community in the areas of business continuity, digital media, creative writing, and brand development. She desires to use creative writing and music as universal languages to encounter anyone, at any walk of life, and lead them to their true potential and capability. Not only does she use creativity, but she also employs her experience and business acumen to assist small businesses, churches, and nonprofits on ways to become successful.

For inquiries, speaking engagements, special events, author book signings, music, list of services, and other creative content go to www.christruleseverythingaroundme.com.

ABOUT THE AUTHORS

NEALY GIHAN

Nealy Gihan was born a month early and a little over four pounds during a blizzard in Downers Grove, Illinois. Although she's always been small in stature, she is fierce, especially when it comes to writing. Ever since she could hold a pencil in her hand and form letters, Nealy has loved writing. Growing up, she'd spend countless hours scribbling out plays to perform with the neighborhood kids. She filled dozens of notebooks with ideas and made-up characters. In third grade, Nealy began her writing career with the release of *The Man Who Fell in Love with Kimberly*, a story loosely based on a comic book she'd read and her best friend's crush. The three-page book was passed throughout her elementary school in Mt. Laurel, New Jersey, and even made its way over to the middle school. Then in sixth grade, the story she wrote and shared about a family vacation in Orlando, Florida, received a standing ovation from her class. And later at Hampton University, she received a national award for a column she penned in the student newspaper. This Midwest Jersey girl is a former newspaper reporter and copyeditor who now labors in coastal Virginia by day as a marketing and communications specialist, also runs her own business, *Purple Inked*, and writes fiction by night. Nealy holds a bachelor's degree in mass media arts and a master's in writing from DePaul University. She has written screenplays performed in Chicago and published short stories available through Amazon. Her business, *Purple Inked*, provides editing and writing services for authors, small businesses, and major corporations.

ABOUT THE AUTHORS

When she's not working or writing, Nealy enjoys reading, hanging out with friends and family, and planning her next international short-term missions trip.

For inquiries, speaking engagements, book signings, and other special events contact:
Purple Inked LLC
PH: 757.563.3177
nealy@purpleinked.com

ABOUT THE AUTHORS

DR. SANDRA HAMILTON (HILL)

Dr. Sandra was born in St. Ann, Jamaica West Indies. She migrated to Queens, New York at a very young age (9), and graduated from Springfield Gardens High School. Dr. Sandra was the recipient of a Bachelor of Business Administration Degree from Florida International University, Florida via Baruch College, NYC; Master of Science Degree from Nova Southeastern University, Ft. Lauderdale, Florida; Master of Science Degree in Religious Education from Jacksonville Theological Seminary, Jacksonville, Florida; a Doctorate degree in Ministry from Seminary, Jacksonville, Florida, and a Doctorate degree in Education with Organizational Leadership and Conflict Resolution from NSU, as well. Her Doctoral dissertation focus on society's response to domestic violence. She was a valuable public-school teacher in Miami-Dade County, FL for 19 1/2 years (1988-2007), then relocated to Washington, DC to make a global impact in the Civil Rights Division of the U.S. Department of Justice, where she currently is. She is the mother of three magnificent children, and the grandmother of four, Isaiah (deceased), Jayla-11, Nazian-5, and Jayce-2 months old. Dr. Sandra is a fantastic woman on the move, confident, friendly, and favored by the Lord. She is one who will rally support and is a builder—always establishing strong, resourceful working relationships. She is a woman of rare, outstanding talent and beauty, knowledgeable, articulate, and focused. Dr. Sandra is a true leader, dedicated to improving every organization that she is associated with. Dr. Sandra engages enthusiastically in ventures that create a difference in the world, such as previously being a qualified candidate for City

ABOUT THE AUTHORS

Commissioner. To top it off, Dr. Sandra recently formed her own non-profit organization *Successful Reintegrations*—a re-entry program for ex-offenders returning to the society. She additionally facilitates anger management/domestic violence groups in Virginia. Dr. Sandra's life goal is to utilize her passion for the least, the lost and the left out, and to facilitate change in the development of a lifestyle of increased value.

For inquiries, speaking engagements, book signings, and other special events go to www.smarturl.it/shill.

ABOUT THE AUTHORS

SHANENE HIGGINS

Shanene Higgins is the CEO and Founder of Higgins Publishing. Shanene is also an empowering keynote speaker and purpose birthing coach. She is the author of the *My Life Journal Bible Study Series* for individuals, Bible Colleges and Christian Universities; a twelve-month color-coded Bible Study series created to help students study the Word of God and strengthen their relationship with Christ to fulfill their purpose. She is the visionary, co-author, and compiler of the *Women of Purpose Anthology* and the *Woman of Purpose, Power and Passion Anthology*! She is also an Award-Winning Artist with the release of her first Contemporary Christian EP *Imagine*, with over 680,000 plays under her Artist name, Shaneen Lavette. Shanene was born in Pensacola, Florida, and moved with her family to California at the tender age of seven. She is the mother of one daughter and one son. After being introduced to Christ by a dear friend she met at work, she received Jesus Christ into her heart as her personal Lord and Savior. Shanene then became active in her church home at Acts Full Gospel C.O.G.I.C. in Oakland, California under the tutelage of Bishop Bob Jackson. After she completed Foundation Class, she learned the principles of the Word of God. She later joined the choir and began ministering in song as well as creating curriculums to teach during Vacation Bible School. Shanene continued in ministerial studies at Jubilee Christian Center Bible College in San Jose, California, under the tutelage of Pastor Dick Bernal. After graduating from Bible College, Shanene became the Church Administrator of Global Christian Ministries in Pinole, CA under the tutelage and mentorship of Apostle Irene Huston. Shanene then created the *My Life Journal Bible Study*

ABOUT THE AUTHORS

Journal as a Bible Study Resource for helping members become more consistent with studying the Word of God. She later became an E-Church member of The Potter's House in Dallas and attended a local church in Hayward, California (Revelation International Ministries Founded by Pastor Nicole Shaw) before being released and sent by God to The Potter's House in Dallas under the tutelage and mentorship of Bishop T. D. Jakes & First Lady Serita Jakes. Shanene is passionate about spreading the Gospel of the Lord Jesus Christ through print, music, and on screen for the glory of God the Father!

For inquiries, speaking engagements, book signings, and other special events go to www.smarturl.it/shiggins.

About the Authors

Tasha Huston

Tasha T. Huston is a native New Orleanian, whose writing is influenced by her love of the culture and her upbringing. You can also find bits and pieces of her experiences and self-taught lessons in her writing which she uses to let others know that they are not alone, in whatever they are going through. She was selected to be a featured writer in *Writer's Anonymous*, an online poetry publication, after submitting only one piece of her work. Her work has also appeared in *Nia Magazine*, an online publication geared toward enriching the lives of women of color. She is the author of *No Chumps Allowed: 7 Keys to Activating your Inner Champion* and *Intrinsic Shift: Shifting and Winning in Life*. She is a businesswoman and Founder of *Pendio Enterprise*, an editorial boutique that specializes in taking your scripted works of art and helping you to make it into the masterpiece you want it to be. Her editorial practice is home to many genres from Sci-Fi to Dating/Romance. She holds a B.A. in Sociology from Louisiana State University and both a bachelor's and a master's in Theology and Religious Studies. She currently works in the Social Services Industry helping families and children overcome behavioral problems. She has worked in this field for a decade and enjoys advocating for those who are often misunderstood. In her spare time, Huston enjoys playing with her dog, Dio, going for a run around the lake, cooking, baking, reading, and traveling. When she is not actively engaged in any of the above-mentioned activities, you can find her in one of two local dance groups swaying to the rhythm and looking for inspiration with each step. She is currently working on her third book due for publication in Spring 2019.

ABOUT THE AUTHORS

For inquiries, speaking engagements, book signings, and other special events contact:

Pendio Enterprise, LLC

pendioenterprise@gmail.com

ABOUT THE AUTHORS

LEONA JOHNSON

Leona Johnson is a certified etiquette expert, co-author, and motivational speaker. She is also an image and branding consultant, relationship and dating strategist, and certified communicator. She is the Founder and CEO of *Allmannersmatter, LLC.* located in Atlanta, Georgia. Leona has had a passion for helping others all of her life. She is a mother of three adult children as well as many beautiful grandchildren from eighteen to two. She has been involved in her community as well as her church for decades. Therefore, she started her many programs with *Allmannersmatter, LLC.* Her program offers basic through advanced levels of etiquette for the integral development of both businesses and individuals alike. *Allmannersmatter, LLC.* showcases modern fun and engaging courses for all ages. Understanding communication as it relates to your relationships, personal or business is very important, and her role to coach you through it is very rewarding when your needs are met. Leona is the co-author of *Poised Polished Professional: The Experts' Guide for Executive Presence.* She has created an action plan guide that will put your Company above the rest!! Leona's mission is to enhance one's holistic growth and develop ways for you to understand the importance of etiquette, civility, and communication. Her passion is community outreach and making a conscious difference in the lives of others through the coaching services she offers and Community Programs. Her programs also provide teens free training for speaking, presentations, posture and grooming; some courses even focus on volunteering.

ABOUT THE AUTHORS

Leona's hands-on coaching gives her the ability to meet the needs of the clients and the commitment to work on their goals. She serves a great recipe for all her services: *Allmannersmatter, LLC.*

For inquiries, speaking engagements, book signings, and other special events contact:
PH: 412.607.3493
Allmannersmatter@gmail.com

ABOUT THE AUTHORS

NORA MACIAS

Nora Macias is the Founder and CEO of *DiVine Design, by Nora*. Her custom-made Gift Baskets have enabled her to bless some of the most prominent Pastors and Church Leaders. Nora also provides decorating services for themed parties, including handmade silk centerpieces and elegant dessert stations. When she isn't creating, she is busy cooking for *Nora's Organic Kitchen*, where she has helped many women turn their conventional favorite home or restaurant recipe into a healthier, organic version. Having been wounded as a child, Nora grew up knowing she was different. Her brokenness led her to many difficult experiences, not knowing all the while, dark spirits were behind them. Once demonic experiences began to manifest, Nora began her desperate journey for answers, and the process of healing began. Today, Nora has a new name. She walks in freedom and restoration. Redemption is her new best friend. Along with being gratefully married to her first love, Rene, a proud mother of her amazing son, Jimmy and an elated grandmother to beautiful, Paisley-Mae, she is living in victory. The most important aspect of Nora's life today is walking in her purpose. Standing on God's promise that *"Nothing is Wasted,"* she has stepped into her calling, reaching out to women of all ages, ethnicities, and social backgrounds. By sharing her story at women's events and hosting Inner-Healing sessions, Nora has been able to help women with wounded hearts become free and has a burning desire to develop this ministry. Nora is currently in the Inner-Healing Ministry and serving on the Creative Team at Redemption Church, Bay Area.

ABOUT THE AUTHORS

For inquiries, speaking engagements, book signings, and other special events contact:

macias.nora@yahoo.com

Facebook at *DiVine Design, by Nora* for creative services.

Nora's Organic Kitchen for delicious, healthy recipes.

ABOUT THE AUTHORS

LEANDRA MCLAURIN

Leandra McLaurin is a Los Angeles native, born and raised. Ms. McLaurin has always marched to the beat of her own drum and blazed her own trails. She always knew she wanted to help others. Ms. McLaurin graduated from Loyola Marymount University with her Bachelor of Science in Health and Human Sciences (formerly known as Natural Science). She also received her Master of Science in Health Education from Kaplan University. Leandra is a Certified Health Education Specialist (CHES) through the National Commission for Health Education Credentialing, Inc. (NCHEC). Driven by her love for life and service to others, Leandra is currently working for the *Black Infant Health Program* in the City of Long Beach as a Health Educator. There she facilitates group and case management for prenatal and postpartum women who identify as African-American to provide social support, empowerment, and stress-reducing techniques for them to have a better birth outcome. Along with her work with BIH, Leandra has also started her own Health and Life Coaching business. Her passion is to help women overcome self-esteem and body image issues by helping them love the skin they are in and showing up powerfully in all areas of their lives.

For inquiries, speaking engagements, book signings, and other special events contact:
Leandra McLaurin Coaching,
PH: 323.596.7276
Leandramclaurincoaching@gmail.com

ABOUT THE AUTHORS

JUDGE SHIRLYON MCWHORTER

Judge McWhorter is the president of *Motivate Worldwide* and founder of the Sister Success Summit. She is a transformational keynote speaker, trainer, and coach. Whether it is a keynote, a breakout session, or an onsite training, you will be captivated by the judge's enthusiasm for life. It is no doubt that her life epitomizes the value of unwavering dedication and focus. Her humble beginnings lead her from the country town of Wauchula, Florida where she picked oranges after school to the courtroom in South Florida where she served as a role model for the litigants that appeared before her. The Judge also serves as the Director of the Office of Equal Opportunity Programs and Diversity at Florida International University where she currently manages EEO, Diversity and Title IX for the University's 56,000 students and more than 12,000 employees. Judge McWhorter is an energetic professional with a dynamic personality and a strong commitment to public service and diverse communities. She graduated with honors from Bethune-Cookman College and received a Juris Doctorate from the University of Florida Law School before moving to Miami where she served as a County Court Judge. She is an active member of her community dedicated to leaving the world better than she found it: Past President of the Miami Dade Alumni Chapter of Bethune-Cookman University, the Miami Alumnae Chapter of Delta Sigma Theta Sorority, Inc., Greater Miami YWCA Board of Directors, former chairperson of the Miami Gardens Educational Excellence Council, member of the Miami Biscayne Bay Links, Incorporated and a graduate of Leadership Miami. She is also a John Maxwell Certified Coach, Trainer, and Speaker. It is no doubt that this

ABOUT THE AUTHORS

former Judge speaks with authority whether delivering keynotes, summits, seminars or workshops. She consistently does so to rave reviews and standing ovations.

For inquiries, speaking engagements, book signings, and other special events contact:
Shirlyon McWhorter
PH: 305.609.7500
shirlyonmcwhorter.com
judgemcwhorter@bellsouth.net

ABOUT THE AUTHORS

MICHELE MILLS

Andrea Michele Mills is a published author of several books. She is an inspirational speaker, visionary, and entrepreneur, she is the Founder and CEO of *Love In Spite of Women's Bible Fellowship*, where Jesus Christ is Lord.

Andrea is a women's ministry leader and Bible teacher. In 2014, Andrea launched the First Annual Prophetic Women's Crusade that was embraced by the mighty presence of the Holy Spirit, manifested through signs and wonders from God in Heaven. Andrea is an anointed minister of the Gospel of the Lord Jesus Christ and has a heart for every ethnicity of God's people. Her preaching, teaching, and writing style bring a ministry of hope, healing, and deliverance to all. Her message is to inspire and provoke change while speaking and sharing God's Word of truth in love. She truly has a heart of compassion for the lost and hurting souls. She's also working on her first musical stage production. Her ultimate goal is to open up a Transitional Home for women and children and a Residential Home for seniors, specializing in Dementia. Andrea resides in Northern California. She is the mother of two children. One daughter, Adrienne, who suddenly went home to be with the Lord on October 9, 2016; one son, Andre and three grandchildren, Charnell, Ronal III, and Chase Benjamin, all of which, she adores. As a lifetime student of the Word of God, Andrea Michele Mills is perpetually pursuing her education in Theology, with an emphasis in Biblical Studies. She is a voice crying in the wilderness, "If my people, who are called by my name, will humble themselves and pray and seek my face and turn from their wicked ways, then I will hear from heaven, and I will forgive their sin and will heal their land." (2 Chronicles 7:14).

ABOUT THE AUTHORS

For inquiries, speaking engagements, book signings, and other special events contact:

Michele_amills@yahoo.com

loveinspiteofwomensbiblefellowship.org

ABOUT THE AUTHORS

DR. NGOZI M. OBI

Dr. Ngozi M. Obi is an American author, of Nigerian-Igbo descent, whose love for writing has evolved into four published works of fiction to date. Her journey as a writer began in response to her search for a genre of books with an inspirational message that seamlessly tackles the complexity of life's concepts. Craving such ingenuity allowed her to tap into her vivid imagination and create tangible characters that most people can relate to. She also found that delving into writing served as an escape and a way to deal with her late mother's illness and subsequent passing. *Love's Destiny*, her debut novel, is an intriguing tale of love lost and found. Her second novel, *When Dreams and Visions Collide*, is an uplifting tale of fulfilling dreams despite arduous challenges. Her third novel, *Love's Legacy*, continues the quest of true love in a riveting sequel to her first novel. Her latest body of work, *Land of the rising sun: A Fictional Tribute to Biafra*, chronicles the Nigerian-Biafran war, through the eyes of a young and impressionable female nurse whose ideas of how life should be, are well beyond her times, in a historical fiction tribute. Most of Dr. Obi's books are creatively imagined from life's organic flow and aim to inspire adults of all ages. Her books are currently available in three different formats; hardcover, softcover and digital download through most online booksellers. They can also be requested at traditional brick and mortar stores. Dr. Obi resides in the love-filled state of Virginia where she currently serves the community through pharmacy practice. In her spare time when she is not busy writing books, she enjoys traveling, experimenting with different food recipes, frequent spa escapes, shopping, and reading.

ABOUT THE AUTHORS

For inquiries, speaking engagements, book signings, and other special events go to www.ladyofdestiny.com.

ABOUT THE AUTHORS

BEVERLY REYNOLDS

Beverly Reynolds is the mother of a vibrant 8-year-old boy. Since the day he was born via adoption, she has made it her mission to take her son on several vacations with family and friends. This has included the Caribbean, hiking in national parks, camping in local private and state parks and even cruising through Alaska. She works hard to provide him with many life experiences through scouts, sports, and even working on homework assignments. Together, they also like to work on several service projects to benefit the community. In her spare time, Beverly enjoys competing in beauty pageants from the local to the global level. Through pageantry, she has the ability to be a positive role model for women and moms of all ages. She believes it is essential to empower women to be 'their personal best.' Beverly also enjoys writing, drawing, photographing, and visiting new places. Beverly's first heart-warming book about adoption, *Here and There: Loving You Always*, is a book that is now available worldwide to inspire perspective adoptive and birth parents to have an open dialogue, perhaps with boundaries clearly communicated, for the benefit and comfort of the children involved. She believes that adoption is a beautiful gift for all family members involved. Any child in or surrounding the adoption journey must know that there are hosts of people who love them unconditionally!

For inquiries, speaking engagements, and book signings, go to www.smarturl.it/breynolds.

ABOUT THE AUTHORS

TIFFANY RICHARDS

Tiffany Richards is a writer, blogger, licensed therapist who specializes in trauma, and a child welfare administrator with over twelve years' experience in family systems. She graduated from The Ohio State University with a bachelor's in sociology and the University of Dayton with a master's in clinical counseling. She launched wordsbytiffanyrae.com in July, a personal development blog that provides a forum for women to address common lessons in life and love. Tiffany believes that our primary mission should be to become our best selves and live our best lives. She uses her testimony, professional knowledge, and her passion for writing to provide insightful encouragement. Tiffany strives to help normalize conversations addressing mental health and trauma issues that are prevalent in our society. When she isn't writing or working, Tiffany enjoys spending time with her precious three-year-old daughter, Talia, and practicing self-care. Tiffany has loved to write for as long as she can remember; however, her journey as a writer has been interesting. As a child, Tiffany would create her own greeting cards, song lyrics, and short stories. She recited her first original poem at age 12 and won several essays, poetry competitions in her teens. Writing was such a significant part of her life and identity. This was until her early twenties when she had some challenging life experiences that distracted her from her gift for over a decade. Then in 2016, she could feel God urging her to begin writing again. She didn't understand it, but instantly, her love affair with words was rekindled, and her purpose was revealed. Through it all, she has learned to trust her talent and the timing of her life.

ABOUT THE AUTHORS

For inquiries, speaking engagements, book signings, and other special events contact:

Tiffany Richards
PH: 614.507.7718
Trich620@gmail.com

ABOUT THE AUTHORS

JASMINE SPRATT-CLARKE

Jasmine Spratt-Clarke is a wife, mother, and owner of theJSbrand – where she helps authors tell their stories through manuscript editing. Jasmine also provides marketing solutions to small business owners. Jasmine holds a bachelor's degree from the University of Mississippi and a master's degree in public relations. In her spare time, you can catch her traveling, reading, or thrifting. Jasmine knows first-hand that when we release fear, we can thrive and live more purpose-filled lives. She's passionate about helping other young women to pursue purpose and to have faith.

For inquiries, speaking engagements, book signings, and other special events contact:
Jasmine Spratt-Clarke
P.O. Box 721
Amory, MS 38821
theJSbrand
jasmine@thejsbrand.com

ABOUT THE AUTHORS

SHAUNIC STANFORD

Shaunic Stanford is passionate about storytelling; she began writing stories as a child. She always had a creative imagination and love for the arts. She played with the idea of becoming an actor and took classes at the Cincinnati Playhouse, where she truly fell in love with writing from an assignment to create her own monologue. Already in route on a different path than her passion, she earned a Doctor of Physical Therapy degree in 2011, from the College of Mount St. Joseph. Inspired by interesting stories from her patients and love for film, she began her journey as a screenwriter. She enrolled in a screenwriter's workshop at the Jacob Krueger Studio and learned the craft. She also took a television comedy workshop taught by Jerry Perzigian (The Jeffersons, Golden Girls), who further fostered her talent through one-on-one mentorship. Shaunic, is currently in pre-production for her short film, *Decide*—a woman trying to have a baby with her husband after three miscarriages must decide what to do after she is raped and becomes pregnant, was a Semi-Finalist in the 2016 Screencraft Short Film Production Fund. It also made the top 50 in the Shoot Your Short competition and made the second round in the Austin Film Festival Screenplay Competition. She currently lives in California, where she enjoys spending time with her family and traveling.

For inquiries, speaking engagements, book signings and other special events contact Shaunic.Stanford@gmail.com.

Quinn Thompson

Quinneckia "Quinn" Nicole Holden-Thompson (born January 17, 1983) is a Mississippi native and one of the first survivors of the rare Kawasaki disease in the state of Mississippi who grew to become a radical Christian woman under the leadership and influence of her parents and mentors, Bishop Joe Holden, Mrs. Penny Holden, and Dr. Tonya McGill. Quinn is known for her outgoing personality and drive to motivate and encourage others by helping them to achieve goals that seem to be unattainable. Quinn is an alumna of Madison Central High School, Hinds Community College, and Liberty University where she studied to become a successful accountant and settled in the vocation shortly after her relocation to Texas. She is also an active member of Antioch Christian Church, under the leadership of Pastor Norris Q. McGill. Thompson currently finds pleasure in mentoring teenagers, spending quality time with her family, watching football, and attending NASCAR races, as well as reading and learning new things. She's the wife to Mr. Cedric J. Thompson, and mother of two growing teenagers. Quinn has recently found pleasure in using her spiritual gift of encouragement to write and author her upcoming book, *The Essence of Purple*, and is also a co-author of the anthology, *Women of Purpose*. She strives to achieve any goal that she sets out to attain and loves to be used by God to be a blessing to others in their time of need. Endeavoring to win unbelievers to Christ, Quinn fearlessly reaches individuals that struggle through life and is unashamed to tell her personal story of how she triumphed and overcame some of the toughest moments of her life with the help of God.

ABOUT THE AUTHORS

Thompson continues to strive in pleasing God by living out His divine word and focusing on fulfilling the purpose that He has placed within her.

Quinn can be reached via email and at the social media sites below:
bookingqnt@gmail.com
qholden1983@gmail.com
Instagram: @justq83
Facebook: Quinn N. Thompson
Twitter: 2Qute27

ABOUT THE AUTHORS

EMEM WASHINGTON

Emem Washington is a multi-passionate creative entrepreneur with a passion for teaching, and that has put her in front of diverse audiences, from K-12 students to law students; attorneys, corporate professionals, church congregations, and online audiences worldwide. She enjoys speaking on issues concerning women, youth and young adults, and shares her own experience of overcoming adversities to encourage and empower her 'tribe' to live out fully alive and purpose-filled lives. Emem has a soft spot for those who are often overlooked or underestimated, including children from disadvantaged backgrounds and single mothers. With a B.S. in Biology, a Juris Doctorate in Law, and an LL.M in Intellectual Property and Information Law, Emem never imagined that she would become an entrepreneur. She preferred the campus life over the corporate life and never thought there was a place for her in entrepreneurialism. She remains a 'serial academic' and loves teaching, *and learning*, a wide variety of topics. Emem combines her experiences, legal training and her voice (singing, writing, and speaking) to inspire and support other visionaries to reach their fullest potential. Her advice and counsel have been sought after for many years. Her projects include her debut album, *Rebirth* (available on all major music outlets), a contemporary Christian/inspirational album focused on planting seeds of hope. One popular song on the album is titled *Flip The Page* that draws on Emem's own story to remind listeners that no matter what their situation looks like, their story is not over. When she is not teaching, researching or leading worship, Emem enjoys spending time with her family, reading and listening to podcasts and music.

ABOUT THE AUTHORS

Emem is happily married to Cedrick Washington and is the proud mother of two boys.

For inquiries, speaking engagements, book signings, and other special events go to www.ememwashington.com.

ABOUT THE AUTHORS

DR. MICHELLE K. WATSON

Dr. Michelle K. Watson is a physician trained in surgery, a translational medical research scientist. She is also a techie, trailblazer, innovator, author, entrepreneur, blogger, designer, been around the world yogi, social agitator, commentator, activist, philanthropist, voracious bookworm, bohemian, bon vivant, supercharged STEM geek, and card-carrying member of the double X chromosome fashionista intelligentsia. Possessing a downtown artistic savoire-faire, Dr. Watson can be found traipsing through New York City's DUMBO, Greenwich Village, or SOHO, reading, coding, traveling, antiquing, visiting art galleries and museums, attending the ballet, meditating, or quietly immersed in deep introspection. As she counts her multicultural, multilingual background as one of many blessings from the Most High, she empathetically utilizes this in her interactions with the socially marginalized and disenfranchised. With a Ford, tough titanium brain and a heart of gold, she is known for specializing in sprinkling wisdom and supergirl magic while leaving a little sparkle wherever she goes. As an enthusiastic and dynamic health professional well-versed in many aspects of medicine, research, and the pathophysiological manifestations of disease, Dr. Watson has cultivated a reputation for dedication, discipline, and determination which precede her in tandem with a work ethic unparalleled in its ferocity. She has engaged in experimental work for the United States Department of Defense and has published and presented her research nationally and internationally. Due to her expertise in wound healing, she has served as guest speaker and presenter at the Estée Lauder Laboratories. Dr. Watson is the CEO and Chief

ABOUT THE AUTHORS

Master Yogi of MeDitation Nation!, a company with an avant-garde approach to nontraditional health and wellness, art, fashion, yoga, and meditation. In the future, she might consider her greatest adventure in STEM to be her custom, private planetarium; where she can sit back, relax, daydream, and perpetually and perennially reach for the stars.

For inquiries, speaking engagements, book signings, and other special events go to www.smarturl.it/mwatson.

ABOUT THE AUTHORS

Dr. Pamela R. Wiggins

A native of Fairfax, Virginia, Dr. Pamela R. Wiggins is a CEO, adjunct professor, author, motivational speaker, Florida Supreme Court Certified Family Mediator, and Certified Arbitrator. Dr. Wiggins earned her Ed.D. in Organizational Leadership from Nova Southeastern University, M.A. in Organizational Management from the University of Phoenix, and B.A. in Psychology from Marymount University. Dr. Wiggins is the CEO/Owner of Wiggins Management & Consulting, LLC a 100% woman-owned certified small minority business specializing in staff training, consulting, family mediation, and workshops. Dr. Wiggins is a faculty member in the College of Business, Organizational Leadership, at Southern New Hampshire University. Dr. Wiggins held leadership positions in higher education as Associate Dean of Academic Affairs and Interim Dean of Academic Affairs. Research interests include adult learning and student retention in online courses. Dr. Wiggins has 15 years of experience teaching in higher education, over 4 years of experience in higher education executive leadership, 15 years of experience in staff training, 11 years of corporate executive level leadership experience as CEO, over 7 years of experience in quality management and auditing, and 12 years of experience in social service programs. Career accomplishments include being Recipient of Cox Media Group *Business of the Week* for the week of January 29, 2018; featured in *Jacksonville Business Journal* 2016, *Women on the Move*; Recipient of *Honored Business Award, Jacksonville's Finest* 2016 Business Profile Series, Folio Weekly Magazine, April 27, 2016; Florida Sterling Council Board Examiner, and Certified Lean Six Sigma Yellow

ABOUT THE AUTHORS

Belt. Dr. Wiggins holds professional memberships with Model Agreements & Guidelines International (MAGI), Florida Sterling Council, Better Business Bureau, National Association for Professional Women and The Sloan Consortium.

For inquiries, speaking engagements, book signings, and other special events contact:
Dr. Pamela Wiggins
Wiggins Management & Consulting, LLC
7235 Bonneval Road, Suite 223
Jacksonville, Florida 32256
PH: 904.477.5814
wmc.llc@comcast.net

ABOUT THE AUTHORS

ERIN WILLIAMS

Erin Breaux Williams was born in Nashville, Tennessee in 1984, and was the first child of her parents. Her father, a dentist and her mother, a public-school teacher, raised her. Both parents positively influenced her to become someone relevant to herself and society. For the most part, Erin's upbringing was quite normal. Her parents divorced when she was in 6th grade. Despite that situation, both parents were very involved in her life. She went on to graduate a year early from John Ehret High School in Marrero, Louisiana. Erin had a life-changing experience when she became pregnant at the age of seventeen. Fortunately, she had significant support from the father of her unborn child, family, and friends. Three days after her eighteenth birthday, she gave birth to her first child. With much support from loved ones and a determination to succeed in life, Erin furthered her education by studying nursing, with the hope of becoming a registered nurse. With hard work and dedication, she graduated from Charity School of Nursing in New Orleans, Louisiana. A few years later, Erin married her high school sweetheart. They now reside in Ponchatoula, LA with their three sons. With her educational credentials, she is currently practicing full-time as a registered nurse. In the search for knowledge and quest to further her career, she decided to advance her education by registering in graduate school for nursing informatics. She is scheduled to complete her graduate studies during the summer of 2018. With her genuine passion and desire to help women realize their own power, she began a blog titled "Femme a` Femme." Through her achievements, she demonstrates the true strength of a woman. Her desire is for every woman to also aspire for the achievement of great things.

For inquiries, speaking engagements, book signings, and other special events contact:
Erin Breaux Williams
erinwilliams@femme-a-femme.org
Femme a` Femme
www.femme-a-femme.org

About the Authors

Deborah Young

Ms. Deborah Young is a follower of Jesus Christ and a ultramodern entrepreneur living in Houston, Texas with her thirteen-year-old son. Born in Voorhees, New Jersey, Deborah's parents moved to North Philadelphia, PA where she was raised. Ms. Deborah is a recognized business owner and leader in the Houston area where she owns a variety of businesses. Ms. Deborah is the Founder/CEO of Lions Group Financial Planning, a financial firm in Houston that provides quality financial services to families and individuals in search of financial freedom, security, and debt control. Ms. Deborah is also the Co-owner of Thru Grace Media, a well-known media company offering digital media solutions to clients for their businesses and brands. After moving to Houston, Ms. Deborah established Imperial Hair Designs, a concierge beauty salon serving women and children in the Houston area. As a faithful member of Greater Works Ministries, Deborah serves inside and outside of the church walls. She loves her church as this was the place that welcomed her as she came to know Christ. Dealing with brokenness, fear, and pain from an abusive marriage that ended in divorce, Deborah saw no hope. Upon learning of Christ's love for her, Deborah dedicated and surrendered her life to Him and has found love, joy, confidence, peace, and healing. Understanding her purpose and the ministry God has placed in her, Deborah founded The Lazarus Foundation, a non-profit Christian organization devoted to helping women overcome barriers from physical, emotional, and mental abuse. The Lazarus Foundation faithfully serves women by providing free guidance and training to women searching for their identity in Christ while gaining confidence, joy, a positive self-image, and self-love. Deborah has a heart for others and those in need. She empowers and inspires women daily to walk in their God-given purpose and fulfill their calling.

For inquiries, speaking engagements, book signings, and other special events contact:
Deborah A. Young
P.O. Box 841578
Pearland, TX 77584
PH: 832.658.1471
Lions Group Financial Planning
info@lionsgroupfp.com

WOP Chapter Registration

WOP CHAPTER REGISTRATION

The *Women of Purpose* Anthology is an anthology that encourages women and girls to never give up on fulfilling their purpose in life. Participants must possess a college degree, own and operate a business and live in the United States.

Story Guidelines:
- Submit a pre-edited inspiring story of 1000 words detailing a life-changing event that impacted you for the better to encourage readers to fulfill their purpose no matter what.
- Story must include how you faced an obstacle that you overcame and how it propelled you to fulfill your purpose in life.
- Must guide the reader into reflection about how they can overcome obstacles as well.
- Must encourage the reader to step out on faith even if they face rejection.
- Must ask the reader a reflection question to propel them to take action at the end of your chapter.
- Must not include illegal, violence, sexual or profane content.

What's included?
- ISBN Assignment
- Cover Design
- Book Formatting
- Electronic Proof
- U.S. Copyright Registration
- Library of Congress Registration

- Softcover, Hardcover & E-Book Availability
- 2 Author Copies
- Author Web Page
- World-Wide Marketing & Distribution

What are the benefits?
- Make Extra Income
- Be Seen as an Expert
- Increase Speaking Engagements
- Encourage Women and Girls Worldwide
- Wholesale Print-On-Demand Services
- Profit 100% of Personal Sales
- Opportunity to Become a Best-Selling Author

What is needed to begin the process?

Sign up to participate in the next edition while space is still available at http://smarturl.it/wopreg.

What if I want to have my manuscript published?

For consideration go to http://smarturl.it/getpublished.

WOP Products

∗∗∗

Thank You for Your Purchase!
Please post a review, and possibly gift a copy or other product to a girl or young woman to encourage her to fulfill her purpose at www.higginspublishing.com.

∗∗∗

Join our mailing list for contests, sales, discounts and rewards.

Women of Purpose Products

These products and more are available at smarturl.it/wop-products.

Women of Purpose Products

Women of Purpose Products

Women of Purpose Products

Women of Purpose Products

Women of Purpose Products

Now that you have the softcover, here are additional formats that you will enjoy as well as the *Women of Purpose* Journal available online at www.higginspublishing.com.

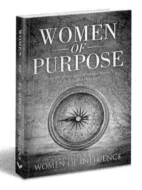 Hardcover Edition

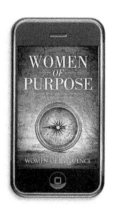 E-Book Edition

Register as an affiliate and earn extra cash by sharing your link! Sign up today at http://smarturl.it/wopaffiliate.

FEATURED ADVERTISERS

Dr. Sandra Hamilton (Hill)
Founder/CEO

Successful Reintegrations facilitates re-entry and reintegration services to men, women, and young adults who are exiting various segments of the judicial system. Organized on November 20, 2017. Our holistic approach is to encourage and support ex-offenders by journeying beside them and their families in an effort to transform their lives and systematically educate them. The program believes that with proper support and assistance, ex-offenders returning to the community will overcome the many barriers of successful living that the incarceration experience can create.

The initial phase of the Successful Reintegrations program includes a training course and leadership development classes.

Successful Reintegrations
SuccessfulReintegrations.org
Office: 703.577.3782

"Serving, Building, and Strengthening Our Community with Re-entry Services."

Denise Warren

Mary Kay
Independent Beauty Consultant

As my customer, I can create your ideal beauty experience. I offer personalized service that fits you. Just tell me if you'd like a one-on-one consultation, a party with friends, a virtual party, makeup tips, skin care advice or free samples. You can always try before you buy. If you prefer to shop online only, by e-mail or phone the choice is yours. I'd love to help you with any or all of your beauty needs. Let's talk!

Specializing In:
Bridal Looks
Makeup Application
Facials
Corporate Gifts
Color Consultations

Destination Wedding & Skincare Specialist

~

PH: 510-776-4284
website: www.smarturl.it/dwarren

Essential Oil Solutions For Health & Wellness!

~

100% therapeutic grade essential oils.

***

Get Products At Wholesale & Earn Extra Income!

Go to:
www.smarturl.it/healthandwellness
for more information & to get started now.

> A percentage of proceeds from purchases will be donated to Sarcoidosis Research.

CPSIA information can be obtained
at www.ICGtesting.com
Printed in the USA
BVHW042145090119
537490BV00008B/48/P